AF606836

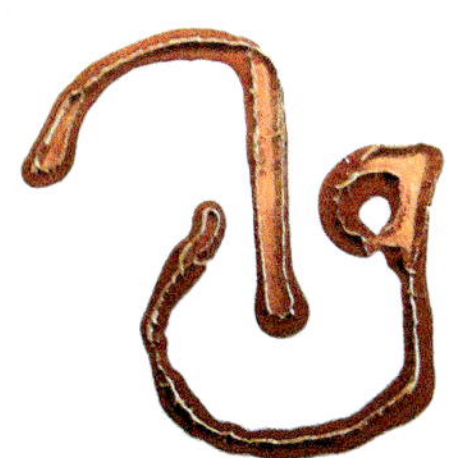

FACES OF THE GREAT MASTERS

Techniques from the Golden Age of Art

Tom Griffith

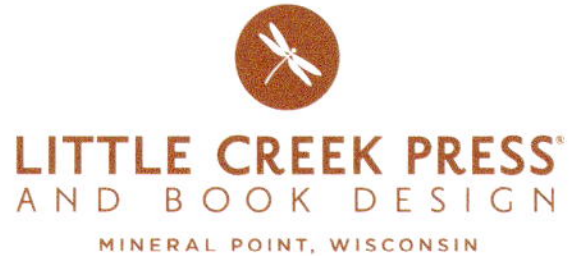

Copyright © 2022 Tom Griffith

Little Creek Press®
A Division of Kristin Mitchell Design, Inc.
5341 Sunny Ridge Road Mineral Point, Wisconsin 53565

Book Design and Project Coordination: Little Creek Press and Book Design

First Printing
June 2022

All rights reserved

No part of this book may be used or reproduced in any manner
whatsoever without written permission from the author.

Printed in the United States of America

For more information or to order books: www.littlecreekpress.com
To contact the author: griffith-oils.art

Library of Congress Control Number: 2022909060

ISBN-13: 978-1-955656-22-1

Disclaimer: The statements in this book are my opinions, based on general knowledge gathered from my observations, readings, and personal experience applying pigmented linseed oil and turpentine onto wood panels. These are the same type of wooden panels often used by many of the great masters. Wooden panels offer a "permanency" that canvas never can. If you disagree with anything I have said or simply have an alternative point of view on some of the statements made, feel free to visit my website at griffith-oils.art or griffith-oils.com to contact me.

On the cover: Griffith, Tom. 2003. Alkyd oil on wood. 9 in. x 11 in. Author's personal collection.

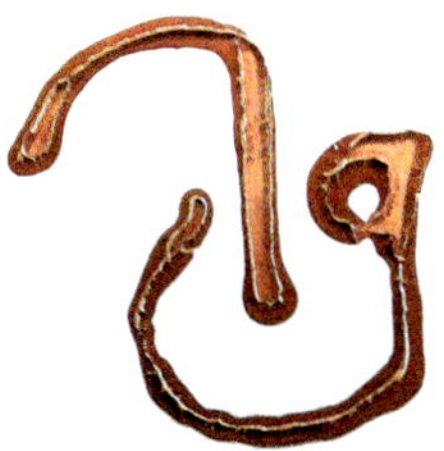

I can't imagine that anyone with many friends could ever find the time it takes to be an artist. For me, art was something I could spend countless hours practicing, filling the time afforded to me when I was a young man. Like many artists, I started with drawing and evolved to watercolors and then pastels and acrylics as the years progressed. Graduating to oils was something I never thought I could conquer. At first it seemed so hard, and the knowledge necessary was so daunting to absorb and master. In oil painting you never "master" anything. Rather, you just get a little better as you complete one more painting. A serious painter always feels something they've done could have been better. Therefore, this book represents what I wish I could have read when I first picked up a brush. It is dedicated to all those who ignored me, giving me the time necessary to practice the art of oil painting and allowing me to leave something behind.

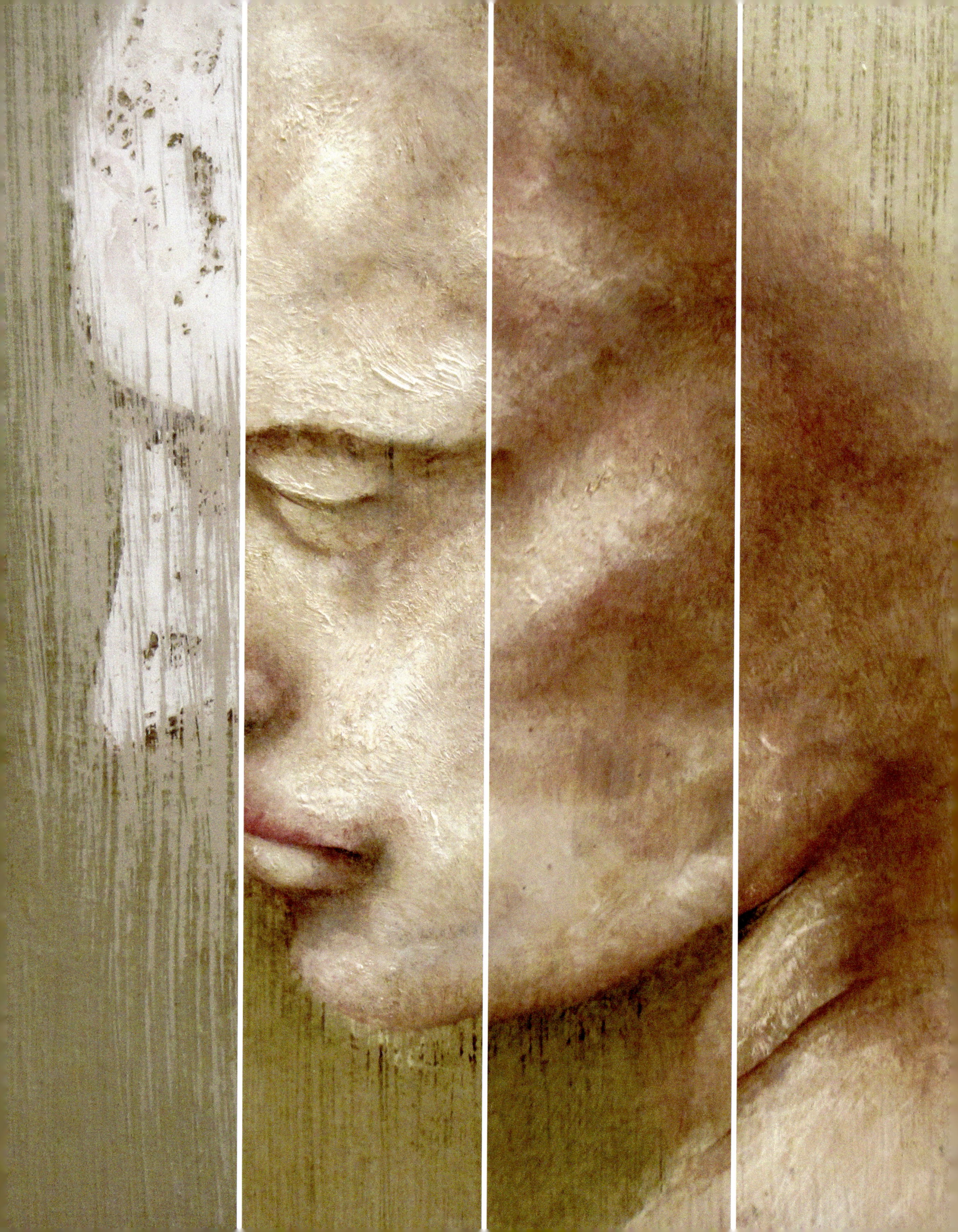

CONTENTS

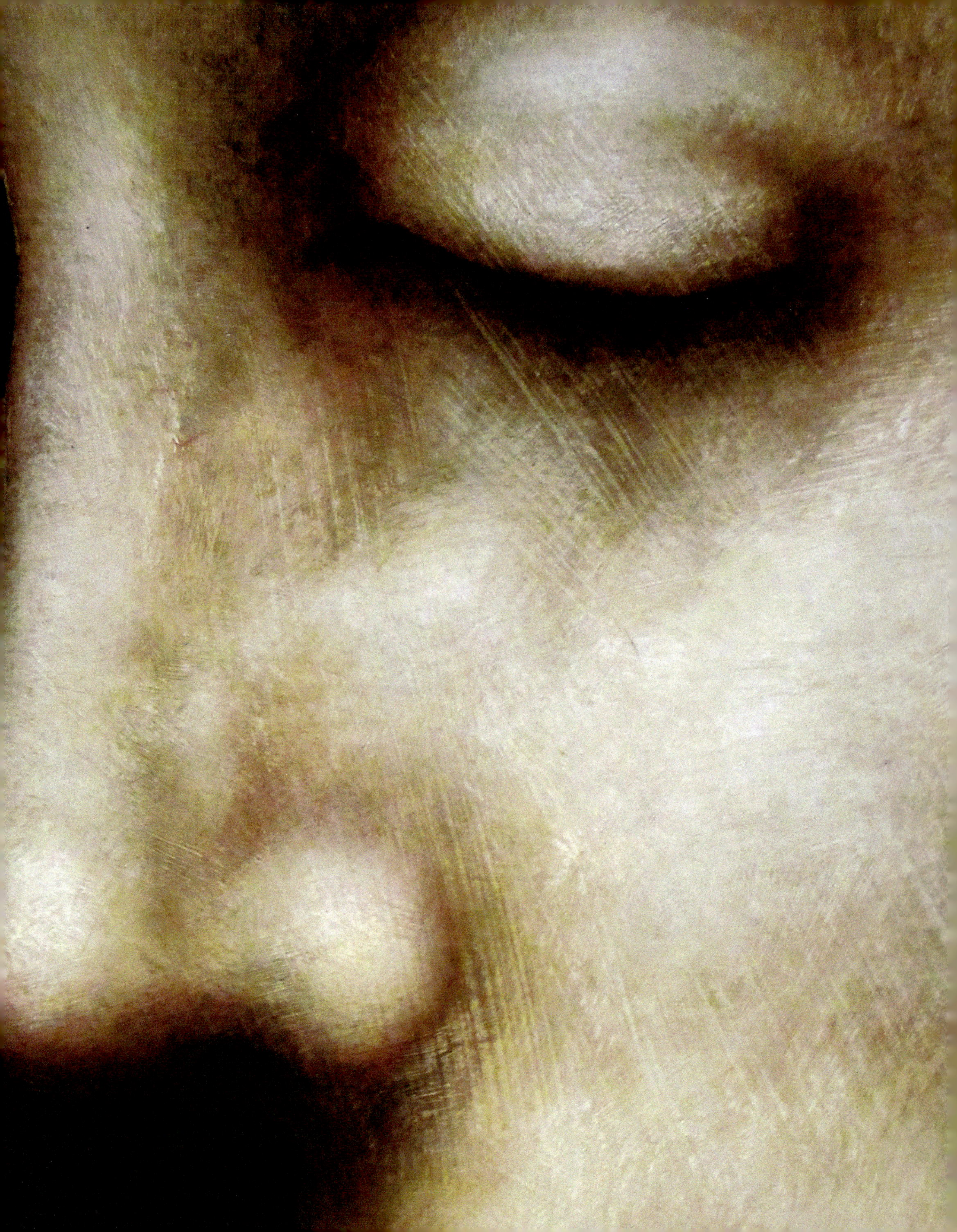

INTRODUCTION

Over the past several hundred years, countless books have been written about art: its history, techniques, materials, individual artists, color theory, etc. These books have been written mostly by researchers, historians, so-called experts—and yes, even an actual artist from time to time. Point being, with so many books and so much information, it is easy to become overwhelmed and, unfortunately, to remember little of what has been read.

Anyone who has ever gone through a book on color theory will know exactly what I have just described. This book too has a section on color theory; but I invite the reader to take it for what it is worth and move on. Many have said that to be a genuinely talented artist, one must be insane. I say, read too many theories on color, and one will become insane.

The purpose of this book is to give aspiring artists a general outline of what is involved in mastering the painting of the human face in a realistic manner. What is written in these next pages are my methods based on what I have gathered through my journey studying the techniques believed to have been used by the great masters of the sixteenth and seventeenth centuries. The book is heavily weighted toward artists from Italy and the Netherlands.

To appreciate the most difficult aspect of realistic painting in oils—that of the human face—one only has to look at how few people throughout history have managed to accomplish this. Although this book focuses mainly on the methods of the Italian painters from the sixteenth century and the Flemish painters of the seventeenth century, it is important to note that without the guidance of painters a century before—mostly Italian—there would not have been what is referred to as the Golden Age of Art given to us by the seventeenth-century artists. A perfect example of this is Michelangelo Merisi da Caravaggio (1571–1610). Caravaggio was, above all, noted for his advancement of the Baroque style of painting through his use of *chiaroscuro* (light and dark), and later what evolved into the technique called *tenebrism* (shadowist). Artists such as Peter Paul Rubens and Rembrandt van Rijn directly benefited from Caravaggio's earlier efforts. It is the style Caravaggio initiated that made possible what we today refer to as "modern painting." This form of realistic painting has been practiced by artists ever since.

The very first book on art was written in a debtor's prison around the beginning of the fifteenth century by Cennino Cennini (c. 1360–1427). At the time, what we now refer to as canvas was parchment and glue over wooden panels or copper plates, plastered and then sanded smooth. The time it took to prepare a single canvas took several days and was usually accomplished with the help of apprentices. This may explain why so many artists re-used their boards when a painting did not turn out the way they intended and why a masterpiece is occasionally discovered underneath a lesser work.

Some of history's greatest and most successful artists were those who broke all the rules of art and then wrote their own. I guarantee that many of the most vocal critics of art have never lifted a brush! Taking note of too many opinions of others only slows a developing artist's flow in gaining skill. A serious painter always feels a piece they have completed could have been better. Reading numerous books on art reveals that many artists use the same subject matter in variations from one painting to the next. That tells me either they were not quite happy with the first one, or they became very comfortable with that scene or pose and painted it again.

This book's purpose is to give a brief but all-encompassing and pointed outline of the knowledge an artist should be equipped with to successfully and convincingly paint the human face.

Unlike many books on art, this book is not unnecessarily long. It hits just the high points of what an artist interested in both the methods of the old masters and the human face should know. It provides the artist with a well-rounded general knowledge of those who have come before. Each photo that I have chosen was placed there for a reason.

My purpose is not to imitate the masters from the Dutch Golden Age but to examine their methods and the materials they used to demonstrate what I believe was their greatest contribution to art.

There are two reasons I have chosen to focus on the *face*. First, the human face is the most difficult thing on earth to paint. The greatest challenge for any artist is to paint a realistic face. Second, if done correctly, the observer of the work pronounces the greatest accolades. Yes, the ego factor. It is that factor that begets the inspiration for the artist to carry on and to go further in perfecting their abilities.

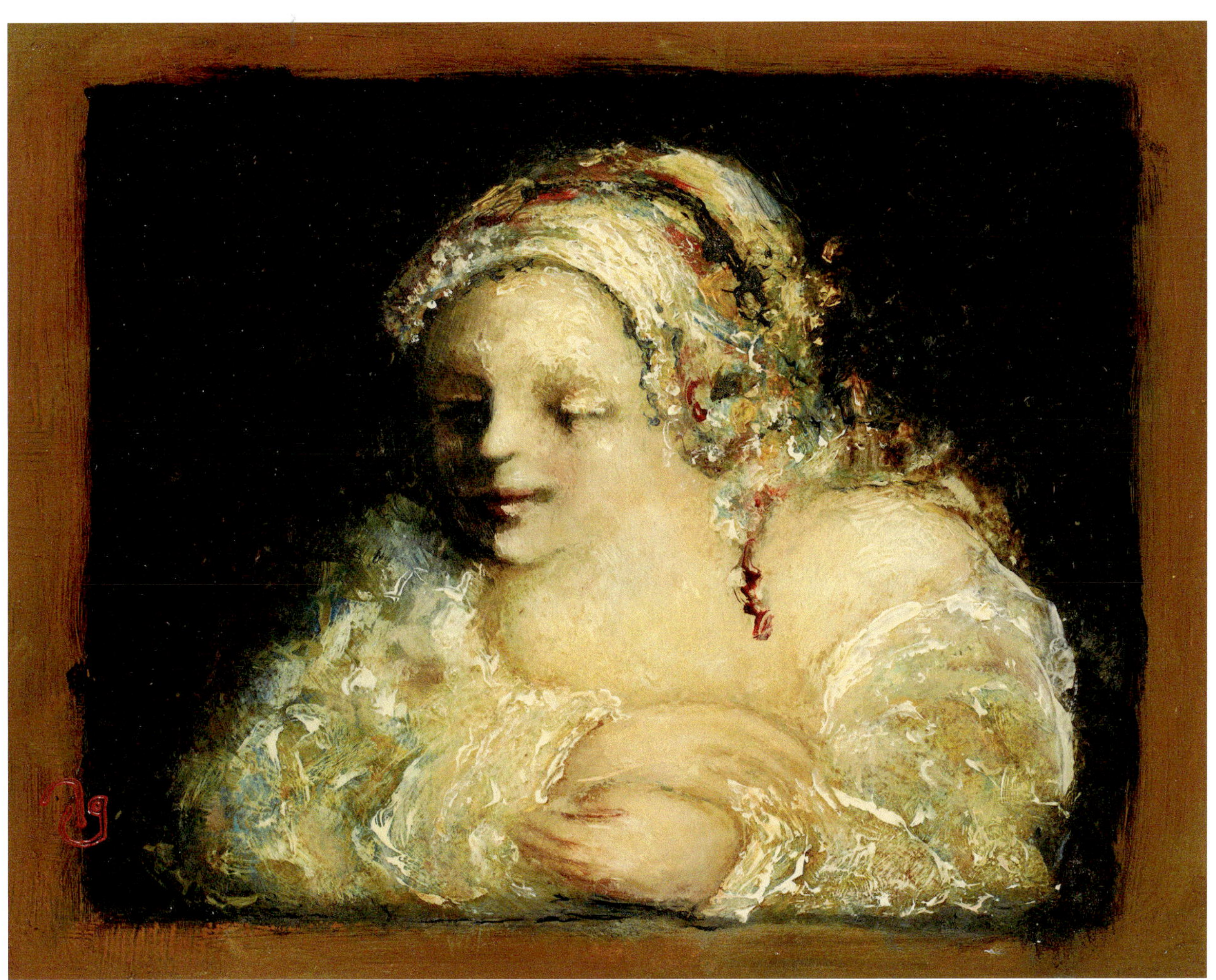

Griffith, Tom.
1976. Oil on wood. 7 in. x 6 in.
Author's personal collection.
Painted with fingers and wooden stick only, no brushes.
(Everyone must start somewhere.)

I have never taken an art class; but rather, through decades of observation of the "great works" of art here in the U.S. and in Italy and the Netherlands, I have come to my own conclusions by way of practice and experimentation with a brush and a tube or two of oil paint. My findings have been tested over time and laid out in detail in this book. Thanks to the help of countless books I have acquired on the Golden Age of Dutch (Flemish) painters, I found the guidance and foundation I needed to emulate what I felt was the type of art I wanted to pursue. Rather than take a path of formal art education, I picked up every book I could find.

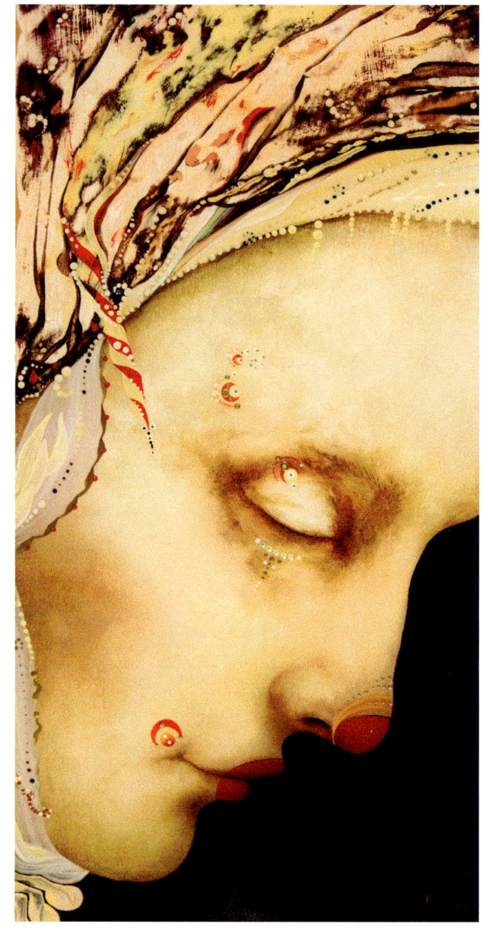

Griffith, Tom.
1985. Oil on wood. 12 in. x 24 in.
Author's personal collection.

Inspiration to be an artist comes from many places. For me, it was in college. As an accounting major, I had no time for painting, although I had always painted as a hobbyist throughout my teens. Prior to that, I drew cartoon characters and experimented with watercolor still lifes. My interest in art was always there. One day a friend of mine from downstairs in the dorm came up to show me the watercolor of a lemon she had painted. Her name was Jill, and she was an art major. Her watercolor lemon was the prettiest thing I had ever seen. After she left that day, I realized that I, being an accounting major, did not even have enough time to paint a simple lemon. The very next day I changed my major to marketing. Marketing was where all the cool kids went who wanted a business degree to make their parents proud while still having enough free time to pursue other interests.

I was always fascinated with the oil paintings of the old masters, but more so *how* they did it. Was there some secret formula they used that was being kept from the rest of us? I sought to find it. That formula, for me was the discovery that by using only three colors and white, I could paint any face. I have used only those four tubes of paint for the past forty years. Being instructed was never one of my strong points. This book shares what I have found out through years of simple observation and practice.

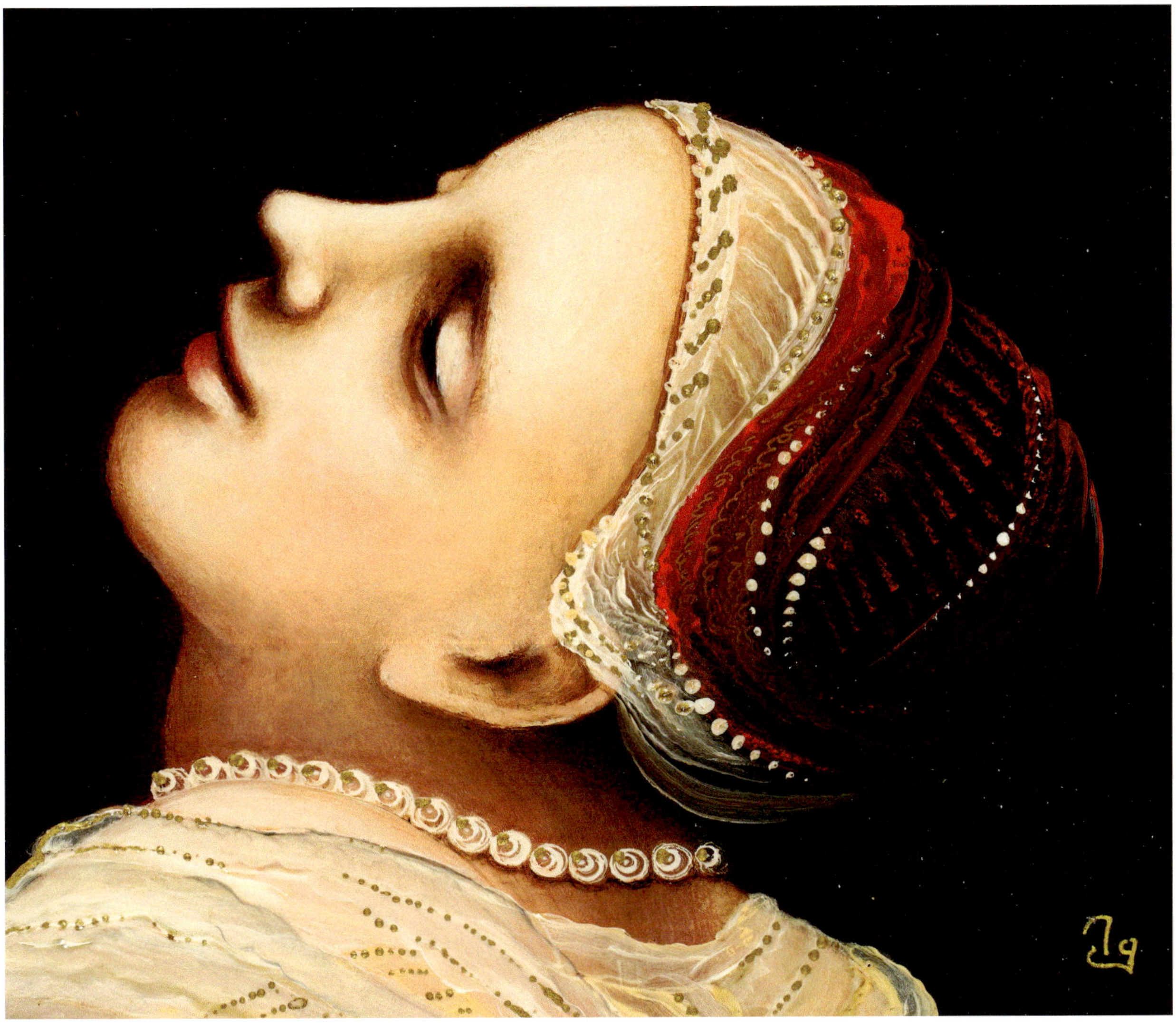

Griffith, Tom.
1984. Oil on wood. 7 in. x 6.5 in.
Author's personal collection.
Inspired by a painting by Antonio Allegri da Correggio
called *Jupiter and Io* (detail). 1532–1533.

Oil on canvas. Kunsthistorisches Museum, Vienna, Austria.

(It was the reaction I received from those who saw my interpretation of Correggio's painting that inspired me to paint only faces going forward.)

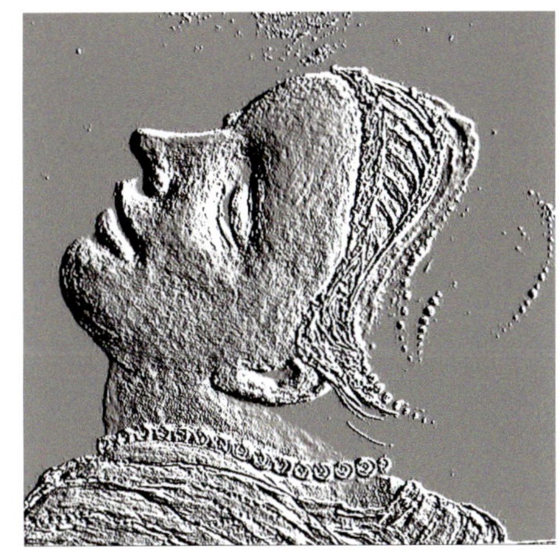

Digitally embossed (at right).

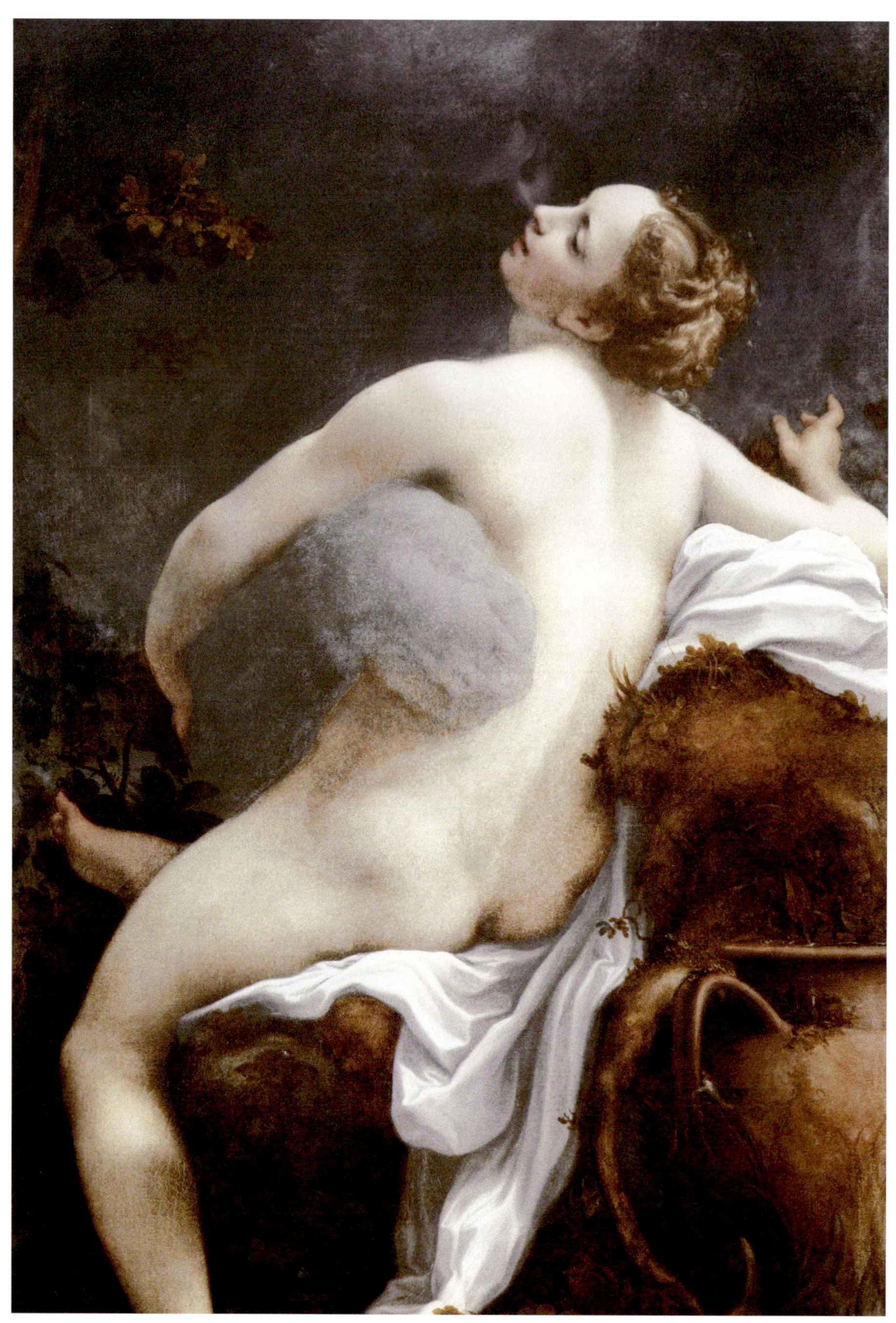

da Correggio, Antonio Allegri
Jupiter and Io. 1532–1533.
Oil on canvas. 27.8 in. x 64.4 in.
Kunsthistorisches Museum, Vienna, Austria.

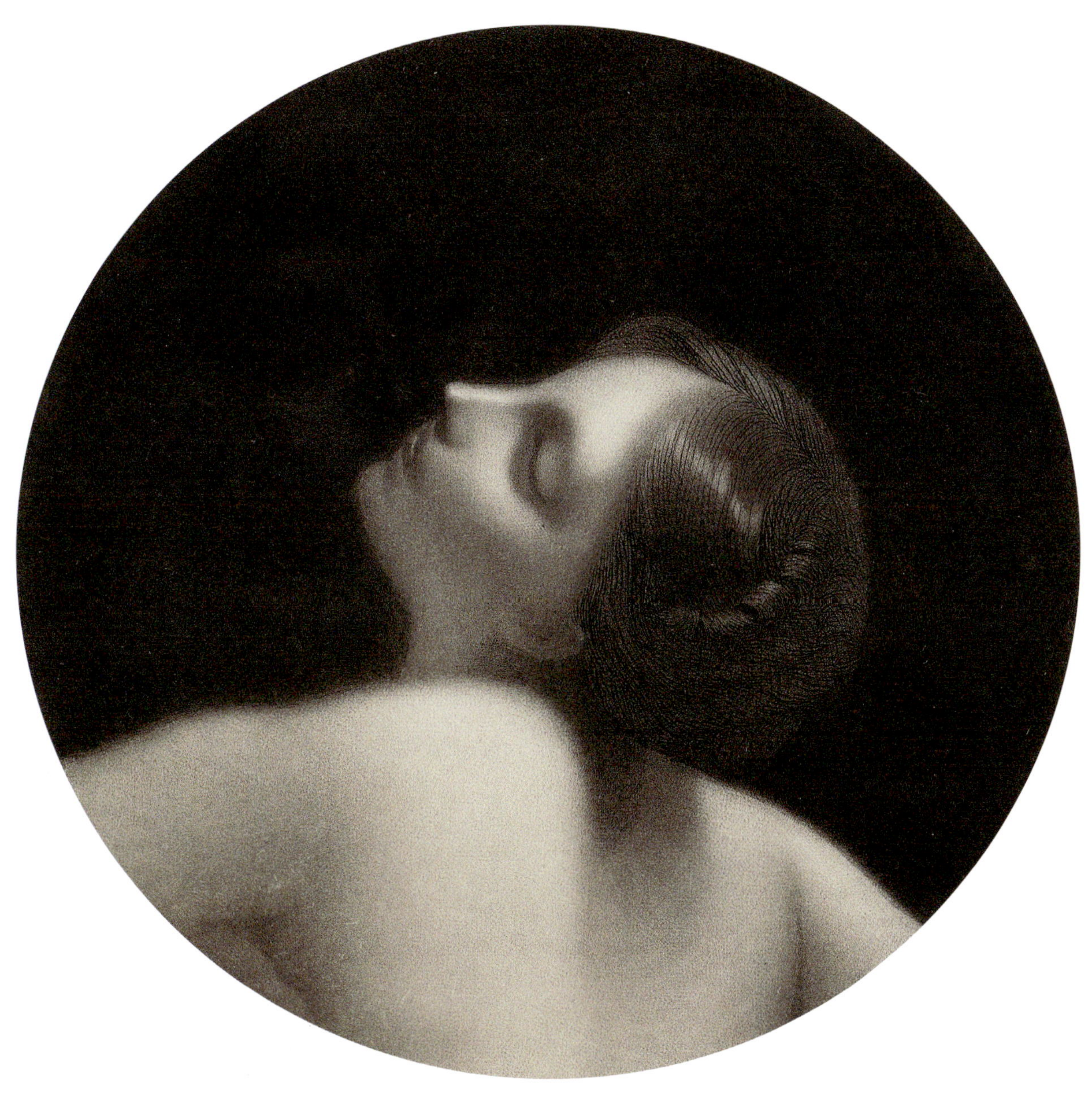

Angerer, L.
Original Lithograph. 1820. 4-3/16 in. diameter.
Author’s personal collection.

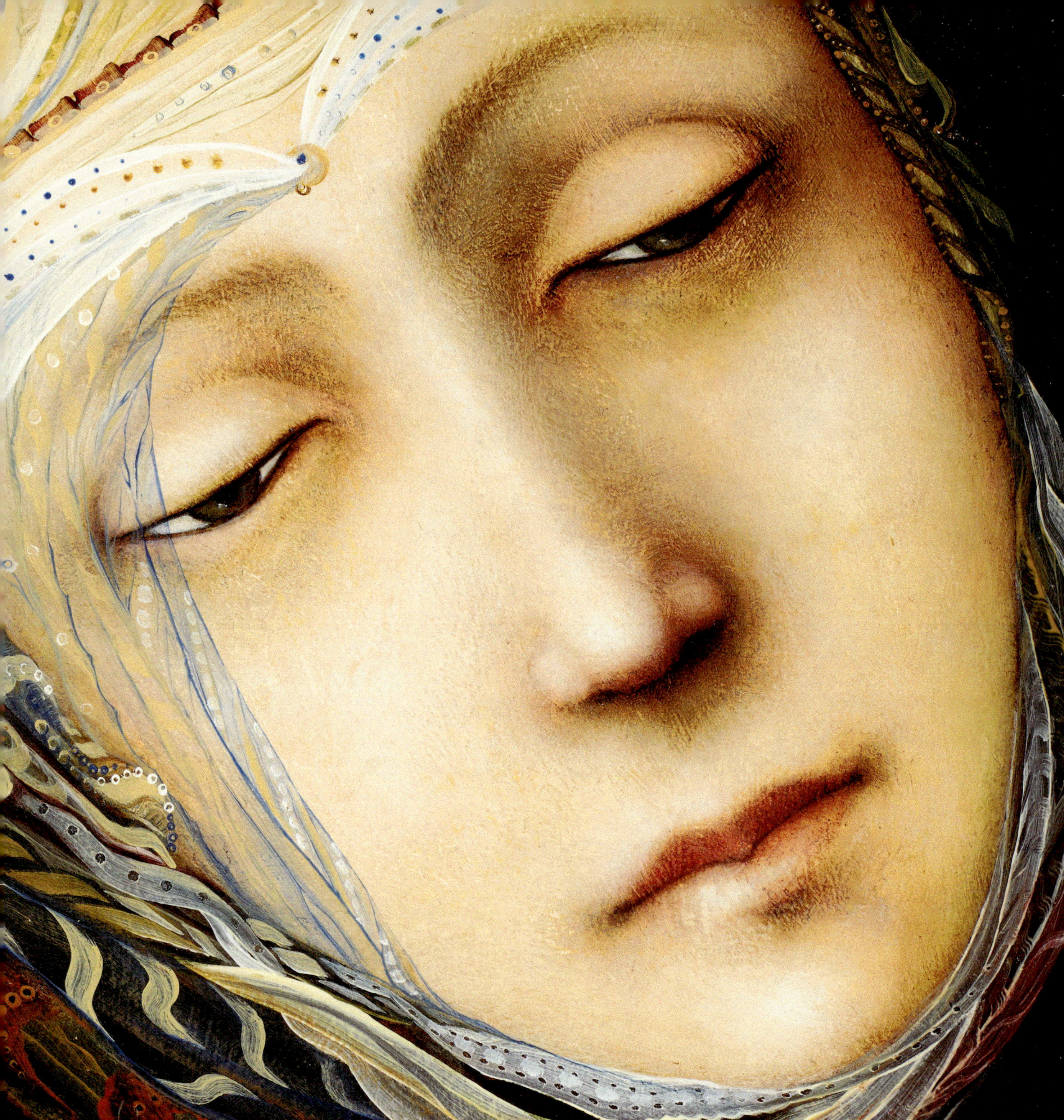

Griffith, Tom.
1990. Oil on wood. 6.25 in. x 6.25 in.
Author's personal collection.

DEFINITIONS

GLAZING

A tinted transparent thin coat of oil, alkyd, or solvent (such as turpentine) to tone down a color. May also be used to create a more 3D (photographic), life-like appearance. Glazing is a wonderful way to paint shadows. Glazing allows light to pass through it, demonstrating its transparent qualities. For example, a yellow glaze over the top of a bluish base color produces a greenish tonality to the object being painted. Glazing allows the artist to portray a look and feel that cannot be accomplished using a brush loaded with paint in an attempt to tone down an area.

ACHROMATIC

Having no color or hue. Blacks, whites, grays, and many browns are achromatic. Achromatic paints are used often in backgrounds to draw the observer's eye to the main subject.

AFTERIMAGE

The opposite color of an image. Staring at the color of an object for a short period of time and then immediately looking at a white surface will result in an afterimage caused by the brain producing the opposite of the original color. For example, stare at a red apple for one minute, then look at a blank white surface. A green image will appear—the opposite or complement of the red apple.

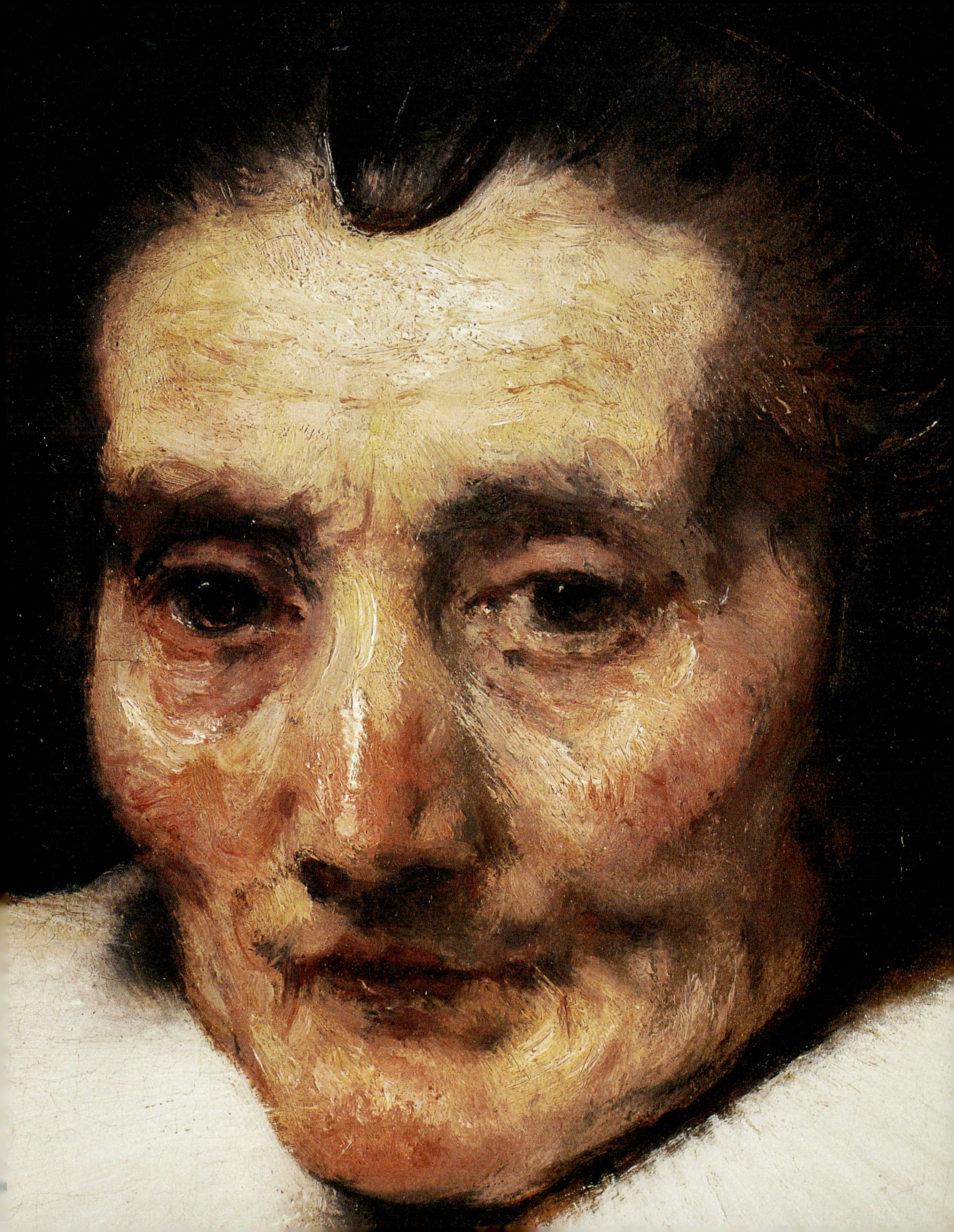

IMPASTO

A technique of laying down heavy underpaint, usually of a very light color that will be a highlight later in the piece. Artists mainly use impasto to demonstrate maximum effect by using thick, brushstroke-lined paint. Later, when glazing is laid down over the top of the impasto, patina and the dramatic underpaint can expose the contrasts of the lighter highlighted areas of impasto. Impasto is an Italian word translating to the word "mixture," representing a thickly laid paint where brushstrokes and/or those of a palette knife are visible.

CHIAROSCURO

Contrast between two colors taken to the extreme for effect. Chiaroscuro is often used on faces. Dutch painters famously used this technique to draw the viewer's eye into the focal point(s) of the painting. The use of chiaroscuro differentiated many great artists from simply good artists, Rembrandt and Vermeer being in the "great" category. However, it was Caravaggio and Albrecht Dürer (German) who were early pioneers of this distinctive style of painting which creates high tonal contrasts.

Chiaroscuro is used in areas of a painting to enable the images beneath the tinted glaze coats to be seen. Chiaroscuro translates to "light and dark." Originally it was a technique taught by the Utrecht School, a Dutch school of art premised on the painting methods of the great master Caravaggio.

This light-dark method of painting was also used by Dutch artist Johannes Vermeer (1632–1675) to express the power of suggestion. Chiaroscuro eliminates the need for the artist to provide exact details in the shadows but instead offers a mere suggestion of their presence. Vermeer was called the master of light and clarity in Dutch art. Rembrandt put down the lightest colors very heavily. He used thin dark brown wash coats for darker colors, such as shadows and backgrounds.

van Rembrandt, Rijn.
Portrait of Margaretha de Geer (detail). 1661.
Oil on canvas. 25.1 in. x 29.6 in.
National Gallery of Art, Washington, D.C.

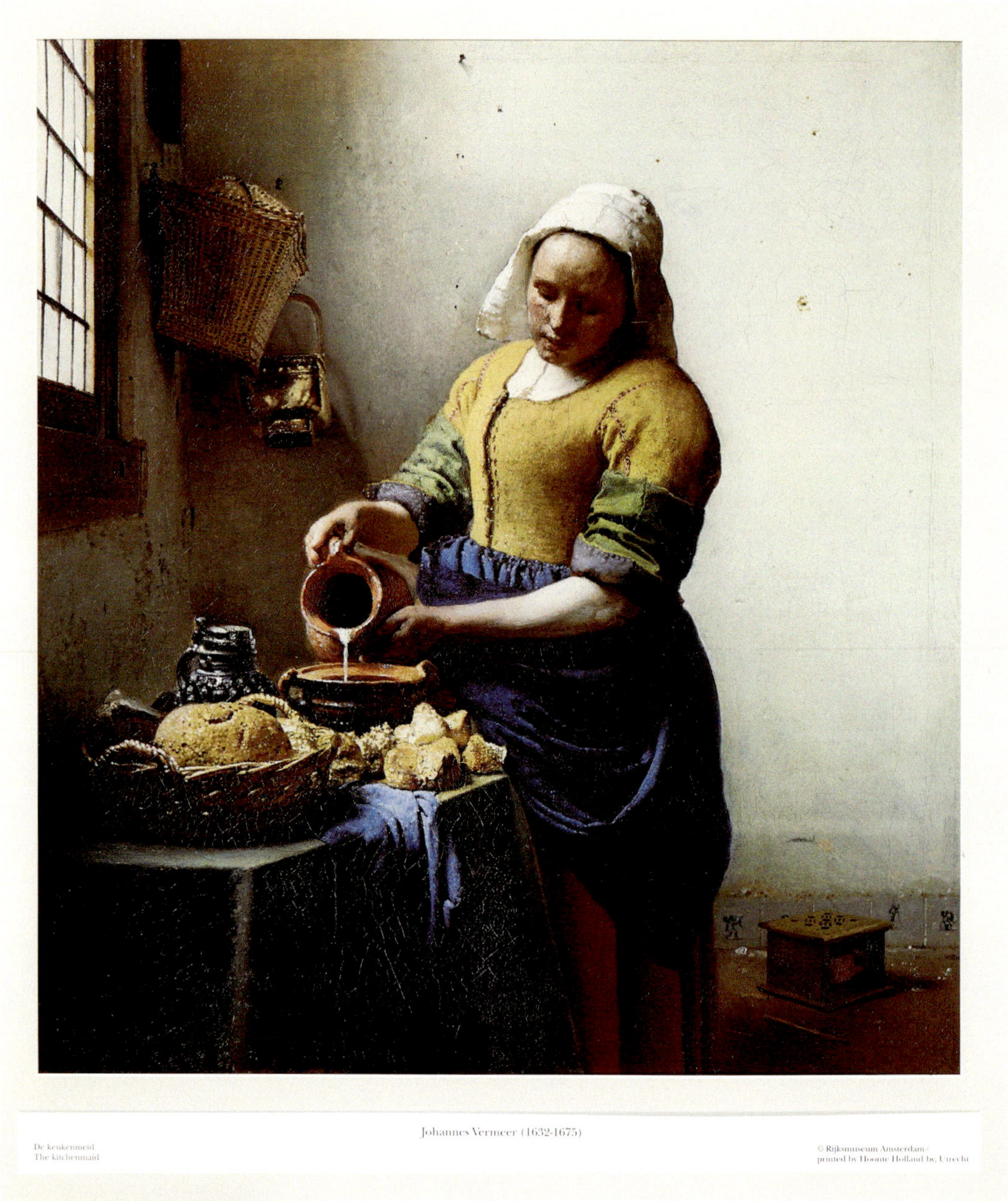

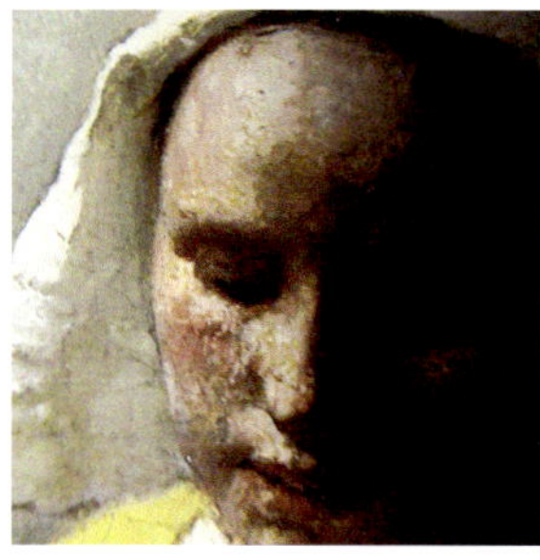

Vermeer, Johannes.
The Milkmaid. 1657–1658.
Oil on canvas. 16 in. x 30 in.
Rijksmuseum, Amsterdam, the Netherlands.

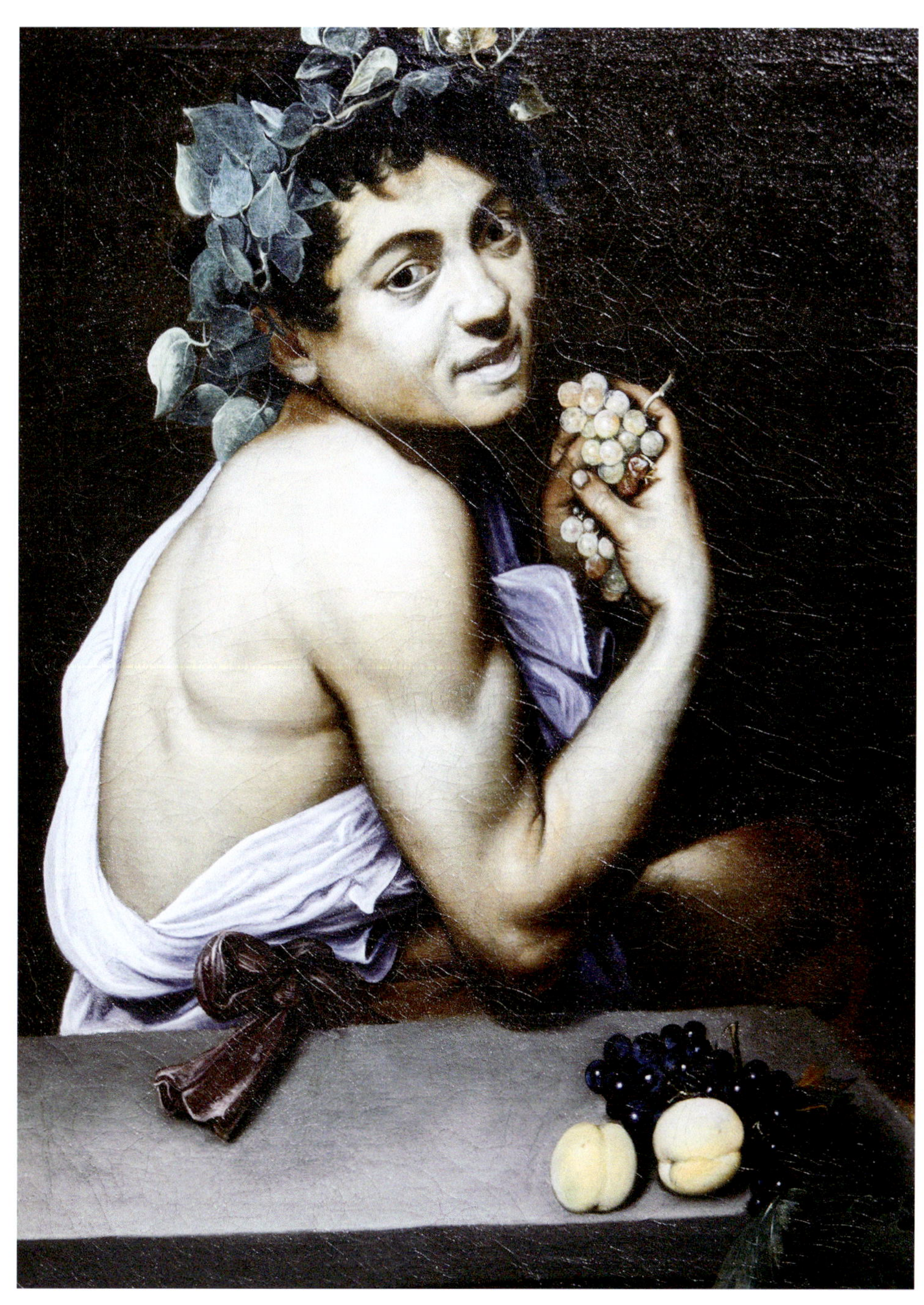

da Caravaggio, Michelangelo Merisi.
Young Sick Bacchus. 1593–1594.
(Self-portrait of Carravaggio at a young age.)
Oil on canvas. 21 in. x 26 in.
Galleria Borghese, Rome, Italy.

TENEBRISM

Dramatic Chiaroscuro. Extreme light and dark contrasts. Most famous for this technique as a "shadowist" was Baroque Italian artist Caravaggio.

OPAQUE

Latin for "dark." In the context of painting, opaque refers to colors that do not allow light to pass through the way a transparent color would. Also referred to as solid colors.

TRANSPARENT

Colors that allow light to pass through. Tinted, a transparent color changes the color underneath it, producing a third color.

da Correggio, Antonio Allegri.
Mystic Marriage of St. Catherine (detail). 1526–1527.
Louvre Museum, Paris, France.

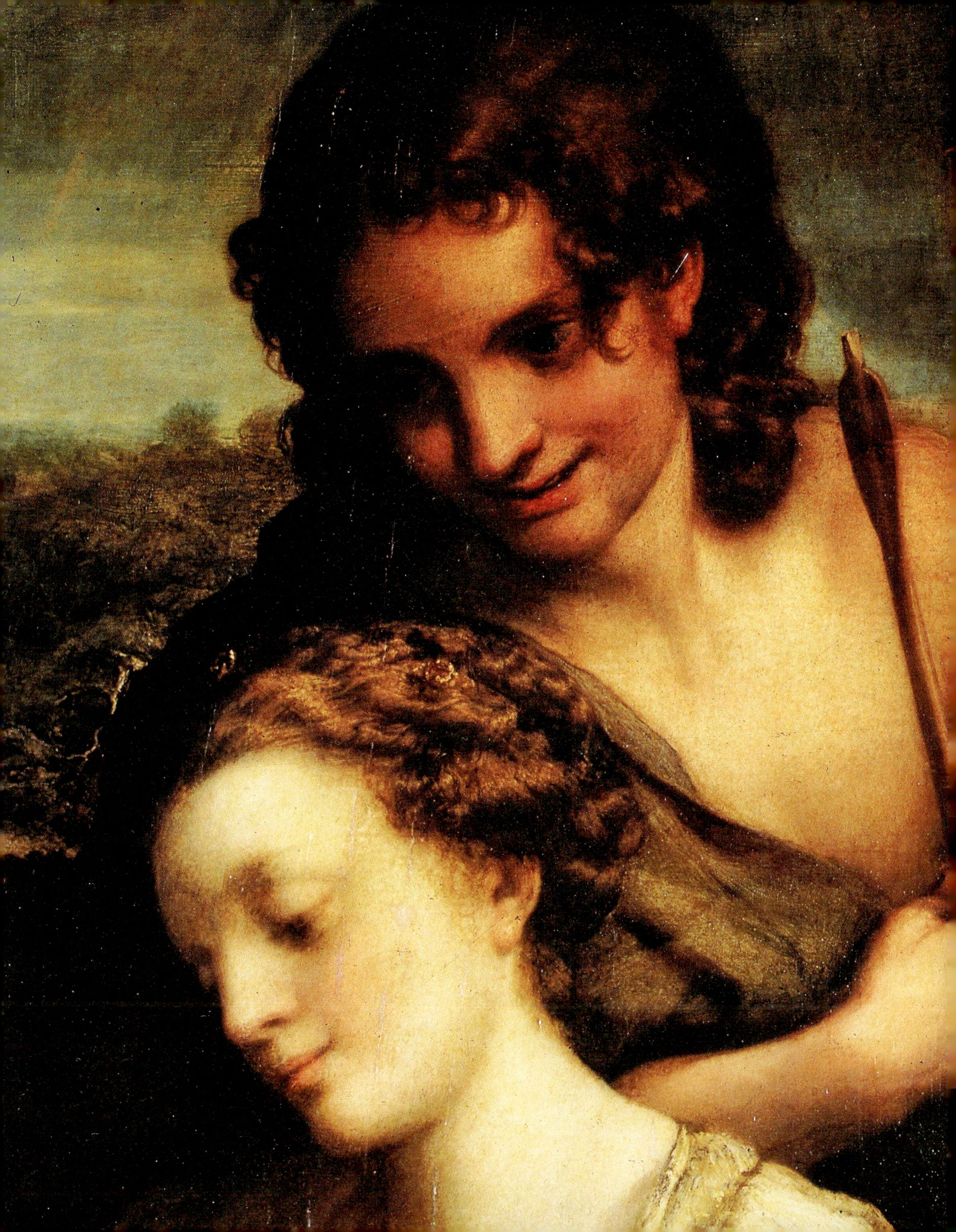

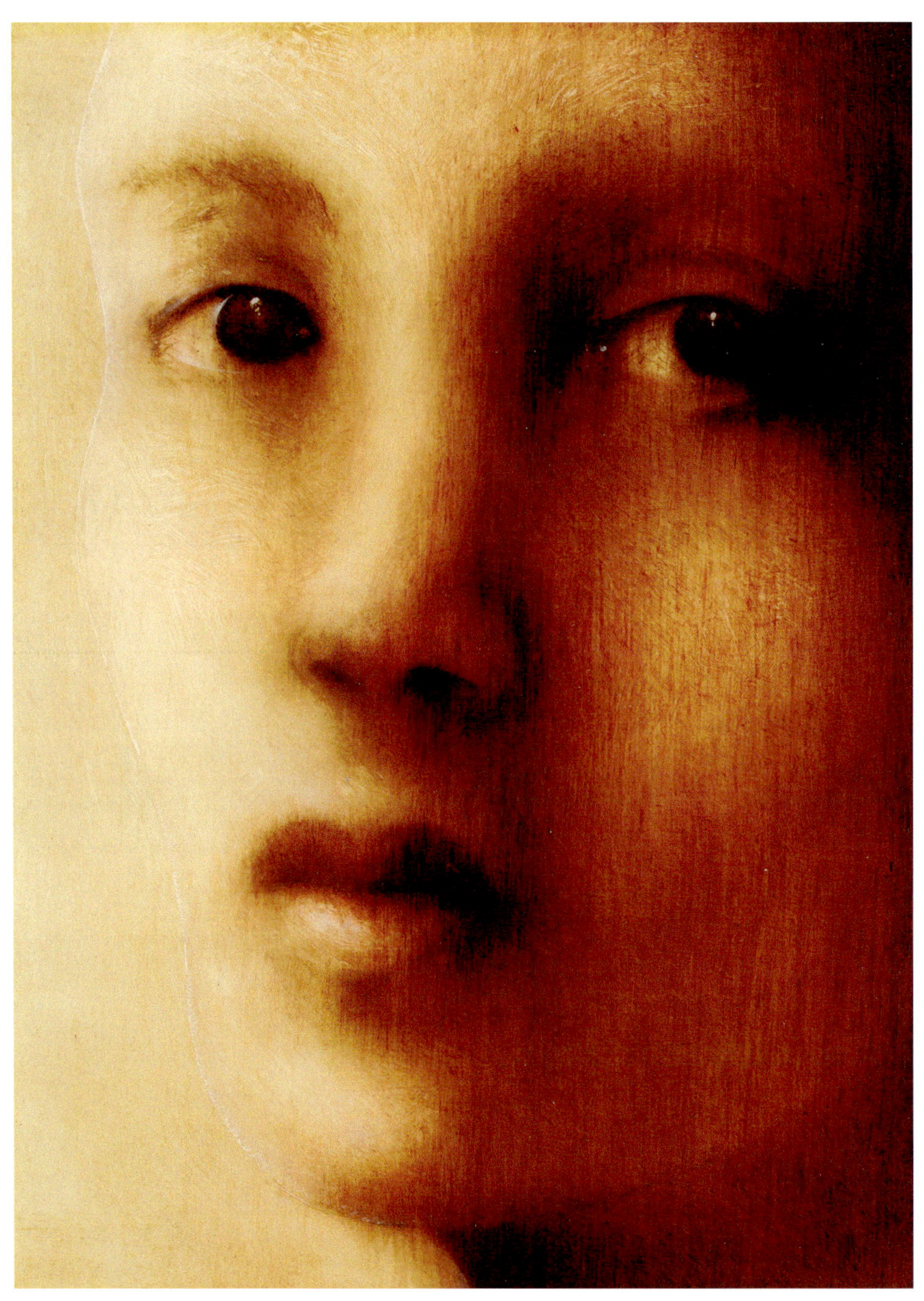

Griffith, Tom.
2010. Alkyd oil on wood. 8 in. x 10 in.
Two colors: alizarin crimson and olive green.
Author's personal collection.

GRIFFITH OIL PUSHING

A technique of using a layer of tinted oil (Liquin) to establish ultra-thin, perfect lines by pushing the tinted (pigmented) oil itself with one edge of the bristles of the brush to form a ridge of tinted oil (forming concentrated lines of pigment), rather than merely painting the lines freehand. An excellent method for creating transparent veiling in very sheer clothing. This technique of pushing oil is an art form all in itself. Using a wedge brush is best for this technique and certainly the best method when painting eyes.

The painting at right is set in a one-hundred-plus-year-old Eastlake mirror frame.

This painting represents two points of interest. The frame itself inspired me to paint something to put in it. Second, it demonstrates that faces do not all have to be painted on a small panel. At almost forty inches tall, this face makes a statement when one enters the room.

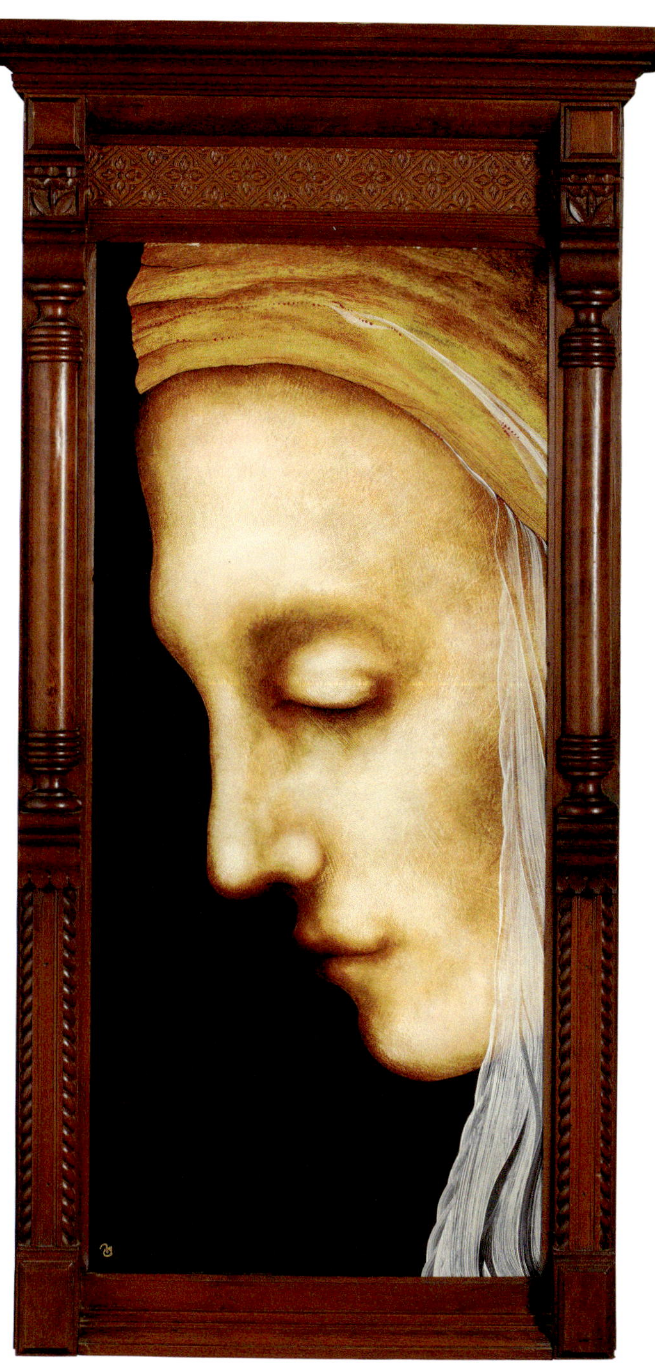

Griffith, Tom.
2001. Oil on wood. 17.5 in. x 39.5 in.
Author's personal collection.

OIL PAINTING

Prior to the invention of what we know today as oil paint, egg tempura was most used when painting great works of art. Artist oil paint is made by mixing equal parts of linseed oil (made from flax seeds) and turpentine and adding pigment (colorant). One can also use poppy seed oil or walnut oil. Pigments are made from plants, insects, natural earth such as silica, clay, minerals or iron oxides, and synthetics (modern day).

DIRECT PAINTING

Most notably practiced by Spanish painter Diego Velazquez, direct painting means trying to achieve the finished color without going through all the steps (i.e., undercoats, mixing shadows, and final glazing). Direct painting attempts to do all of this with a mixing of what the artist thinks the final color is to be on the palette before it is applied. One and done.

Examples of direct painting (right)**:**
Face: titanium white and Naples yellow
Face shadows: titanium white, Naples yellow, and alizarin crimson
Side veil: Naples yellow and alizarin crimson
Head cover: alizarin crimson over tan gesso
Background: olive green and alizarin crimson
Frame: former ornate multi-faceted mirror

Yet another reason to paint on wood. Due to the unusual shape of the mirror that was inside the frame, I carefully removed the mirror and used it as a pattern to cut the wooden panel. Just try to stretch a canvas into this shape!

Note: This painting exhibits no signs of the use of impasto on the underlayers of the face. Additionally, there are no finishing glaze coats. There are times when a picture looks so complete without the normal steps one would take to finish it, that it is time to deem that painting finished.

Griffith, Tom.
2002. Oil on wood. 14 in. x 24 in.
Author's personal collection.

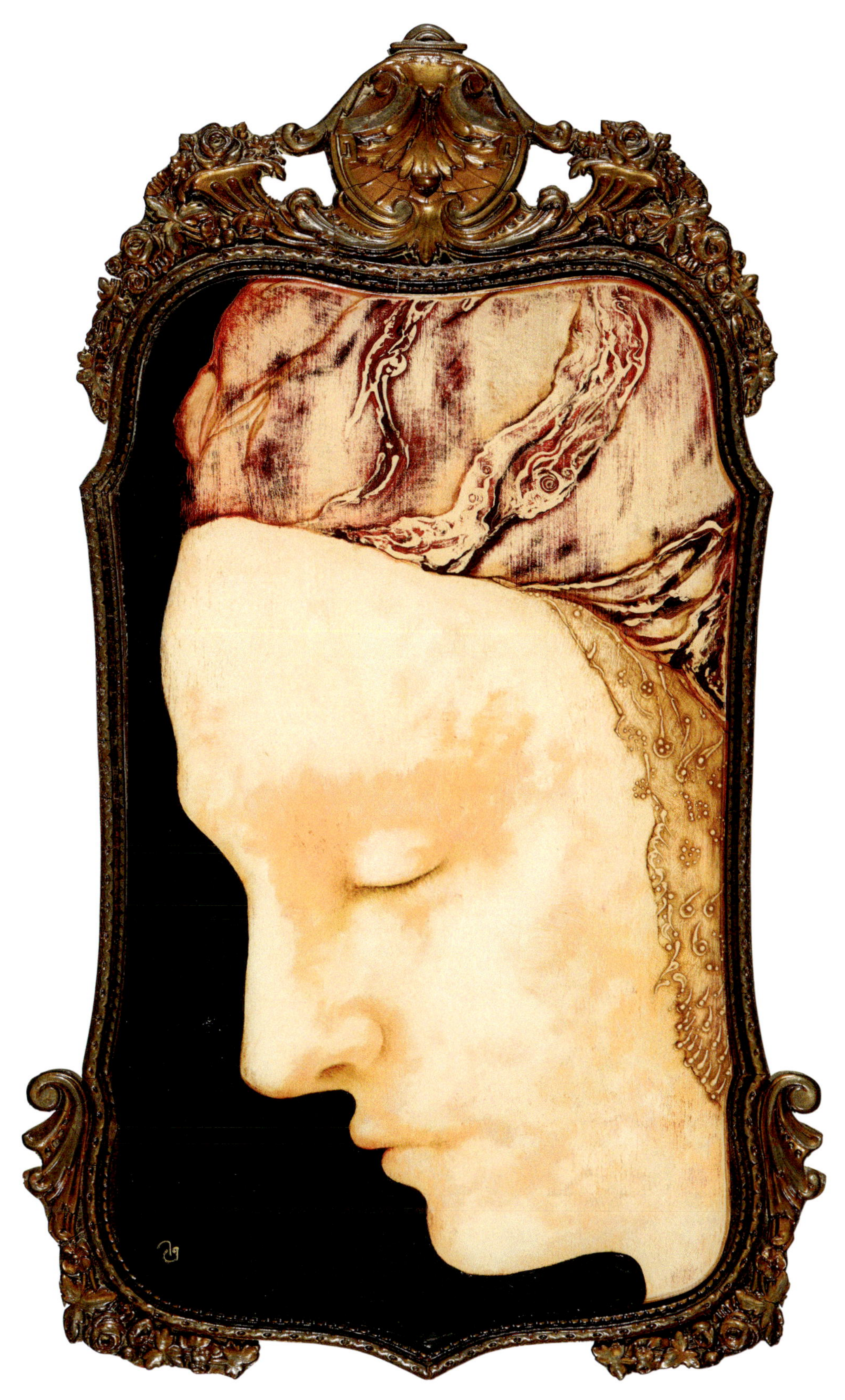

FROTTAGE

A French word meaning to "rub" or "scrub." This allows the lighter (highlight) colors underneath to become exposed by rubbing (sanding) off the layers of the glaze coats on top. This is achieved by using a palette knife or sandpaper.

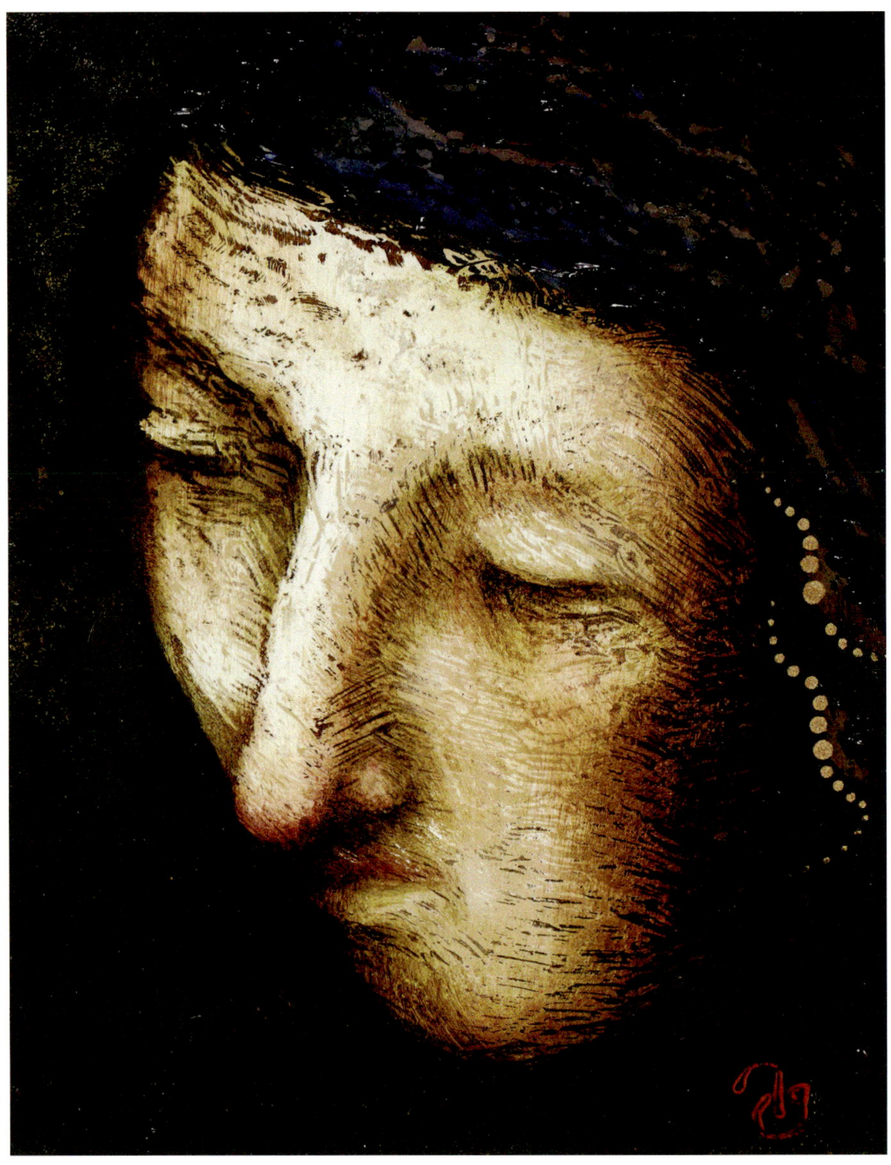

Griffith, Tom.
2021. Oil on wood. 6 in. x 8 in.
Glazing layers removed with a power sander. 400 grit disc.
Author's personal collection.

PLUMBONACRITE

Rembrandt had a secret for thickening his paint to achieve impastos. Plumbonacrite is found in a mineral form of lead oxide. The mineral is heated to 1,112 degrees and the result extracted. Rembrandt discovered this in the mid-1600s. Other artists came about this thickener in the mid-1800s. Exactly how Rembrandt figured this out two hundred years before other artists remains a mystery.

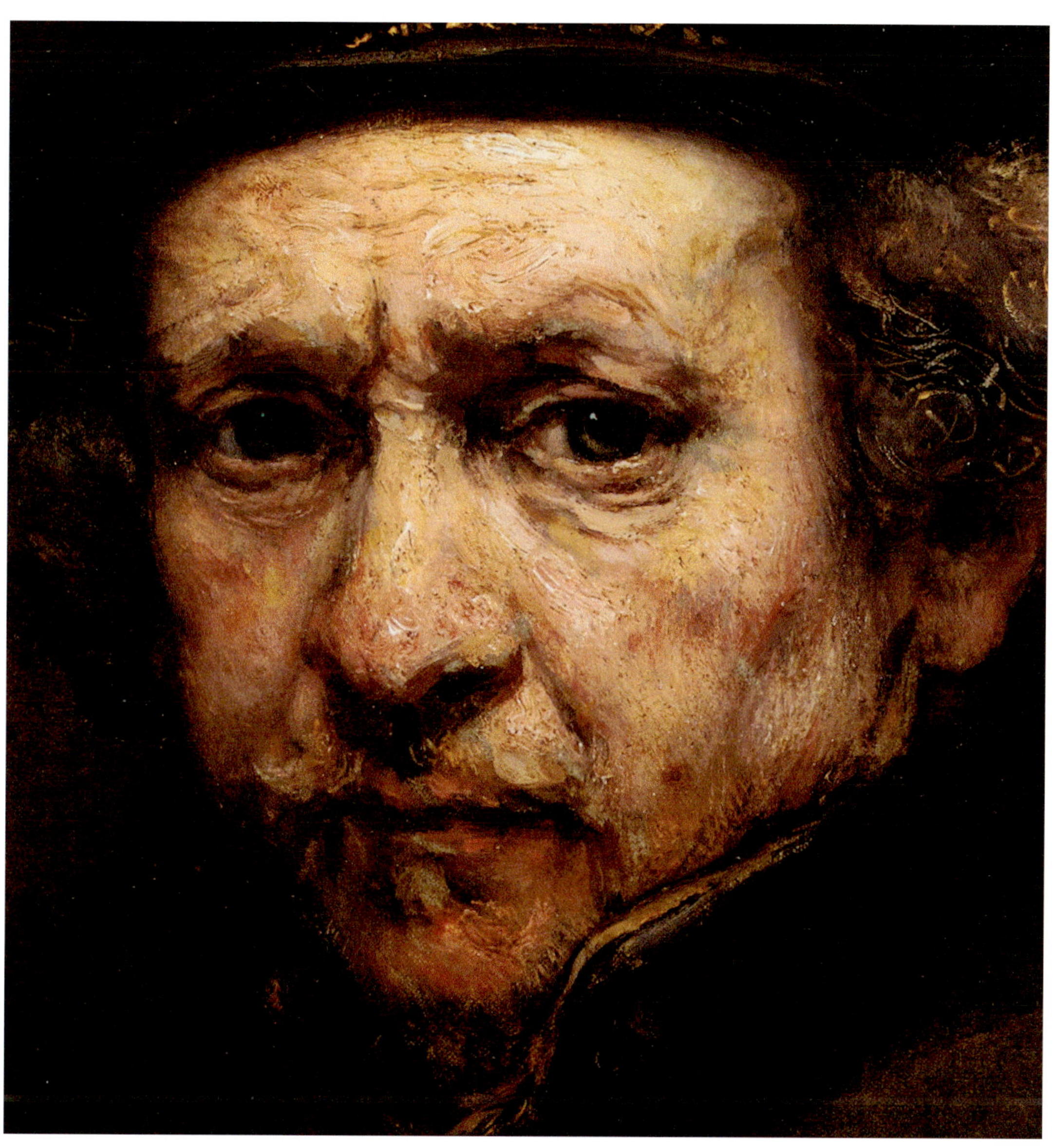

van Rembrandt Rijn.
Self-Portrait (detail). 1659.
National Gallery of Art, Washington, D.C.

ALKYD

Alkyd resin is made from alcohols and acid that allow for quicker drying times when added to oil paints. Often used in thin, transparent, quick-drying glazing coats. Normally two glazing coats a day can be applied. Alkyd is a siccative dryer and is often made from dolomite (limestone), which acts as a drying agent.

There are numerous mediums with which to mix oil paints, all dependent on the end goal. Alkyd medium has the dual effect of acting as a drying agent and the ability to change the consistency of the paint itself. Alkyd pastes will thicken paint for more volume (which is very helpful in creating impastos), whereas liquid alkyds (heated) act as a thinning agent for transparency purposes. This now more transparent paint is wonderful when an artist creates veiling, as seen on the painting pictured here. Veiling takes time and forethought.

The elaborate head cover on the painting at right is basically thin liquid layers of Liquin and alkyd oil paint applied on and off for about four months. Of the approximately fifty layered coats, most likely thirty of them cannot be seen, in that they've been buried underneath the last twenty coats.

Griffith, Tom.
2003. Alkyd oil on wood. 9 in. x 11 in.
Author's personal collection.

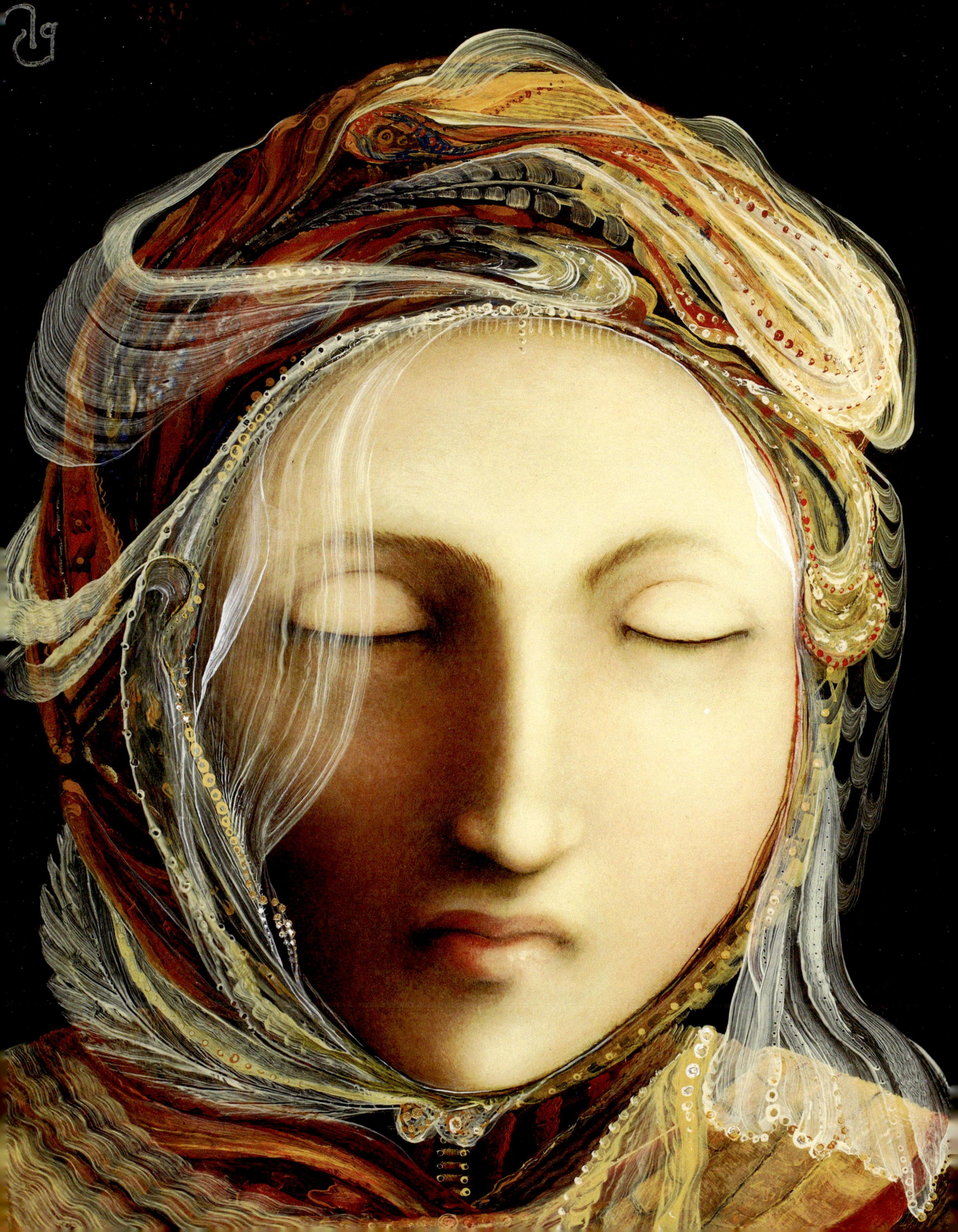

MEDIUMS

Mediums are resins and solvents (such as turpentine) added to oil paint to thin the oil paint and increase its flow to reduce drying times. Or, by increasing the volume of the resin, paint can be further thickened for use with impastos. Alkyds can be added for faster drying time and/or thickening as well.

LIQUIN (made by Winsor & Newton)
Liquin is a painting medium added to oil paint to advance drying time and thin the pigment for easier flow. One can paint an entire painting using just Liquin and a few colors.

THERE ARE TIMES WHEN TECHNIQUE OUTWEIGHS ACTUAL ARTISTIC TALENT.

Some of my best outcomes in art have been what I thought were mistakes at the time. Countless theories have been purported as to the methods used by the great masters. There have even been attempts to tie the artist's surroundings and means of acquiring various pigments (e.g., ultramarine blue made from lapis lazuli, the rarest and most expensive pigment for any artist to purchase) used in the colors they mixed in relation to the period of time in history in which they lived. This is often merely conjecture.

Despite all the mediums on the market to mix into oil paint to change its consistency, sheen, drying time, and transparency, I only use Liquin. Why? Due to the fact I've never had an art class, it was the first thing I ever bought to achieve what I called a glaze to place over the top of the thick layers of paint (impastos) I was putting down first when painting a face. Liquin dries quickly and can be applied many times in a single week. It can also be used to thin colors on your palette so that they flow and spread over the surface of the panel you're painting.

Note: Many mediums can be used for glazing. Turpentine and linseed oil are probably the most common, but poppy seed or walnut oil and turpentine (or any other type of solvent) can be used. Solvents are used for faster drying times and to prevent cracking. Oils are used for a thicker, more luminescent look, but dry much slower.

Up until the eighteenth century, oils were made by the artist mixing the ground pigments fresh with turpentine and linseed oil. Then in 1855, an artist could purchase pre-mixed metal tube paint. The major advantage here for artists is that they could take the ready-to-go paints with them. This was especially advantageous for traveling landscape artists.

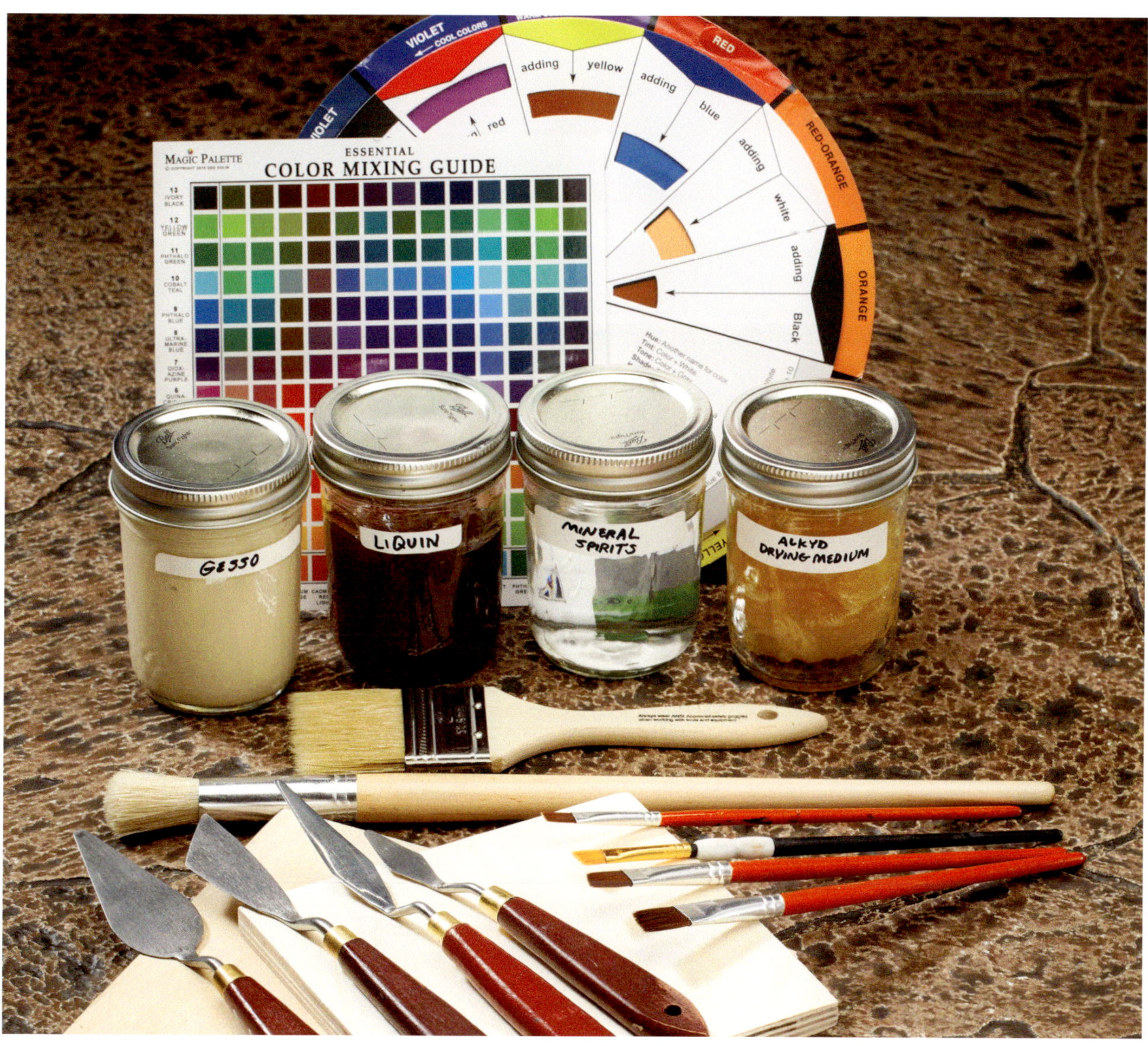

THE ARTISTS

Here is some basic history, with a touch of knowledge about the best painters of the human face from my perspective. It simply comes down to the Italians and Dutch. Many will argue this statement, but everyone has their own opinion. This is just mine.

In striving to become a good artist, knowing a little history of those who came before is both inspirational and provides a guideline as to what may possibly be accomplished.

If one takes the techniques and perspective of the old masters, the Golden Age of Dutch artists (basically the 1600s), one can only better their approach to painting the human face.

When I was a teenager, it was the works of Vermeer of Delft that intrigued me—to the point that I purchased every book ever written about the man, despite how little was known about his life. Shadowed by the popularity and world acclaim of a guy further north in Amsterdam named Rembrandt van Rijn, Johannes Vermeer was, in my opinion, a far more fascinating man. Vermeer, like Rembrandt, died broke. Vermeer was forty-three, Rembrandt sixty-nine.

Johannes (Jan) Vermeer, Delft, the Netherlands, 1632–1675
Rembrandt van Rijn, Leyden, Amsterdam, the Netherlands, 1606–1669

Vermeer, Johannes.
Girl with the Red Hat. 1665–1666.
Oil on wood. 9.1 in. × 7.1 in.
National Gallery of Art, Washington, D.C.

Note: Unlike most of Vermeer's portraits, the focus here is on the hat itself. A chemical analysis has shown that the red hat is painted with an underlayer of vermilion, while the upper layer is a madder lake glaze.

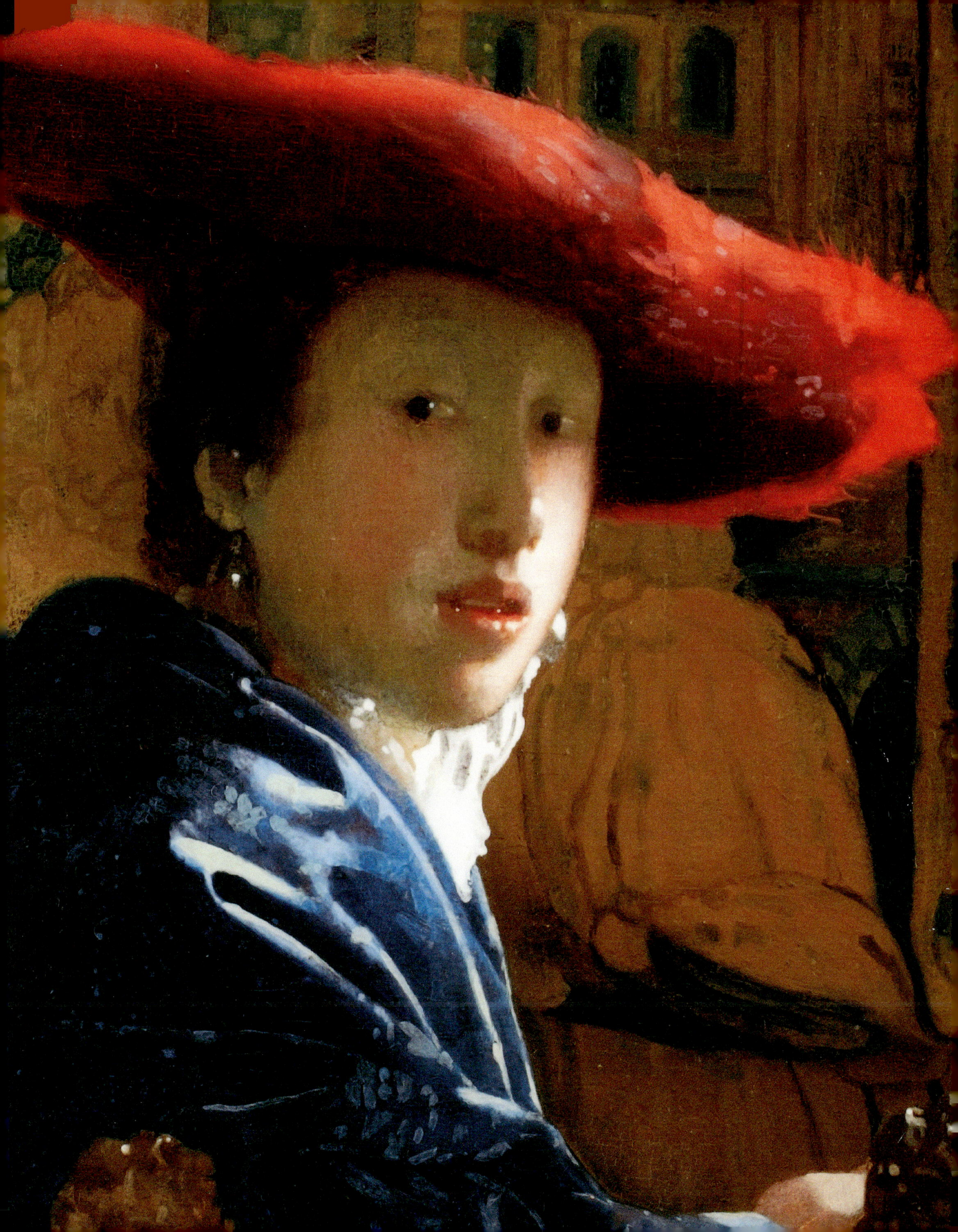

Before any of history's great artists could paint with oil, it had to be invented. Oil paint was invented by Jan (Johannes) van Eyck, a Flemish painter born between 1385 and 1394 in the town of Maaseyck (known then as Eyck), the Netherlands, now part of Belgium. He mixed equal parts of linseed oil and turpentine, plus pigment, of course. That magic formulation is still the way oil paint is made over six hundred years later.

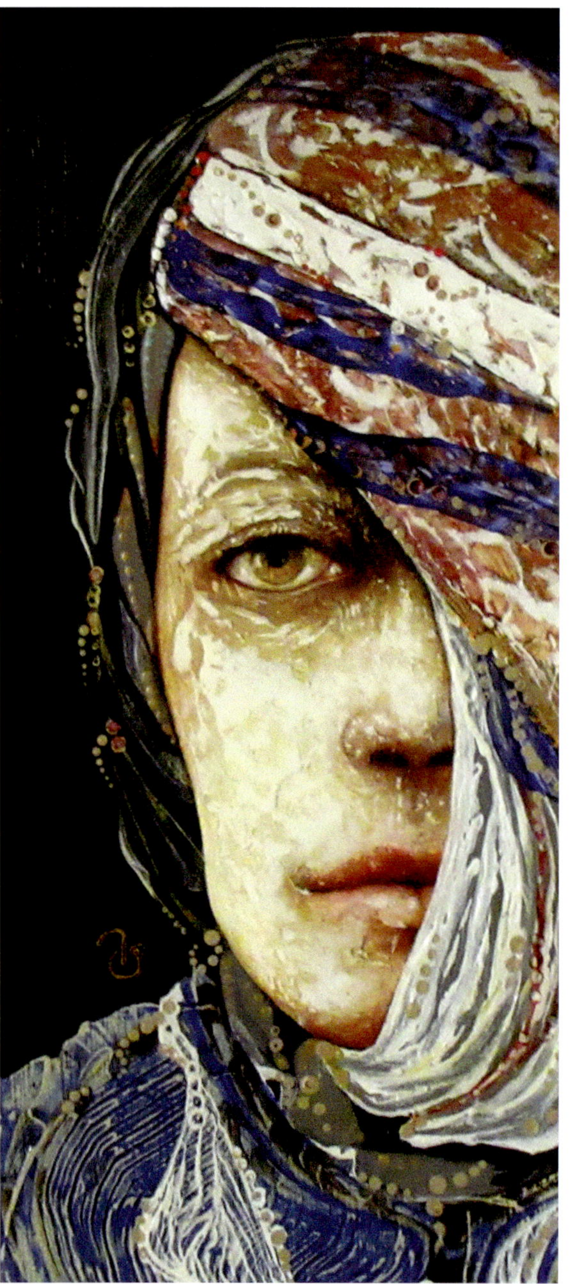

Left:
Griffith, Tom.
2022. Alkyd oil on wood.
9-1/2 in. x 15 in.
Author's personal collection.

Below:
Nine colors were used to paint the eye.

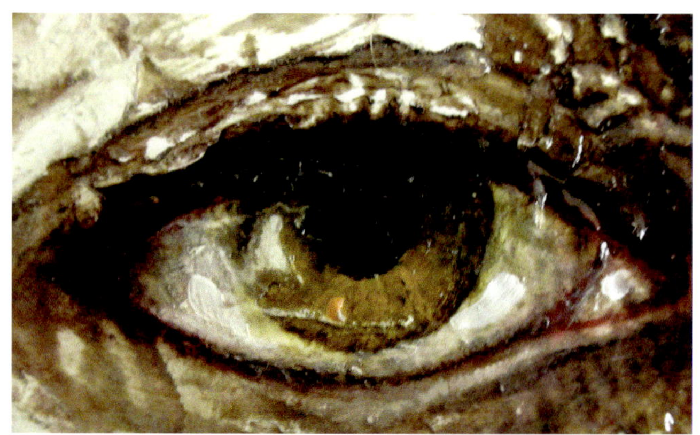

Right:
van Eyck, Johannes.
Man in a Red Turban. 1433.
Oil on wood (oak).
7.5 in. x 10 in.
National Gallery,
London, England.
He often signed his work, "JOHANNES DE EYCK," along with his motto: Als ik kan (As best I can).

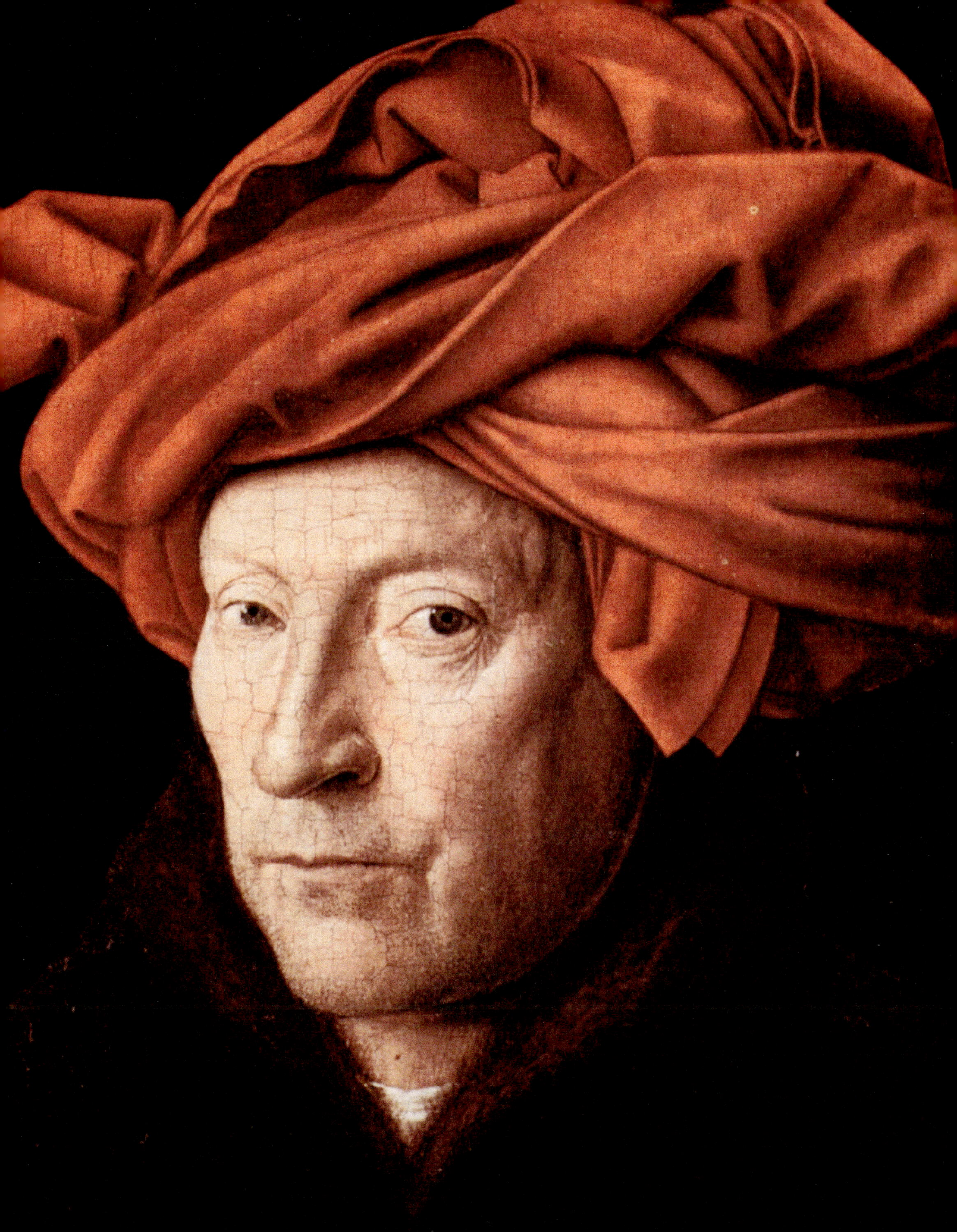

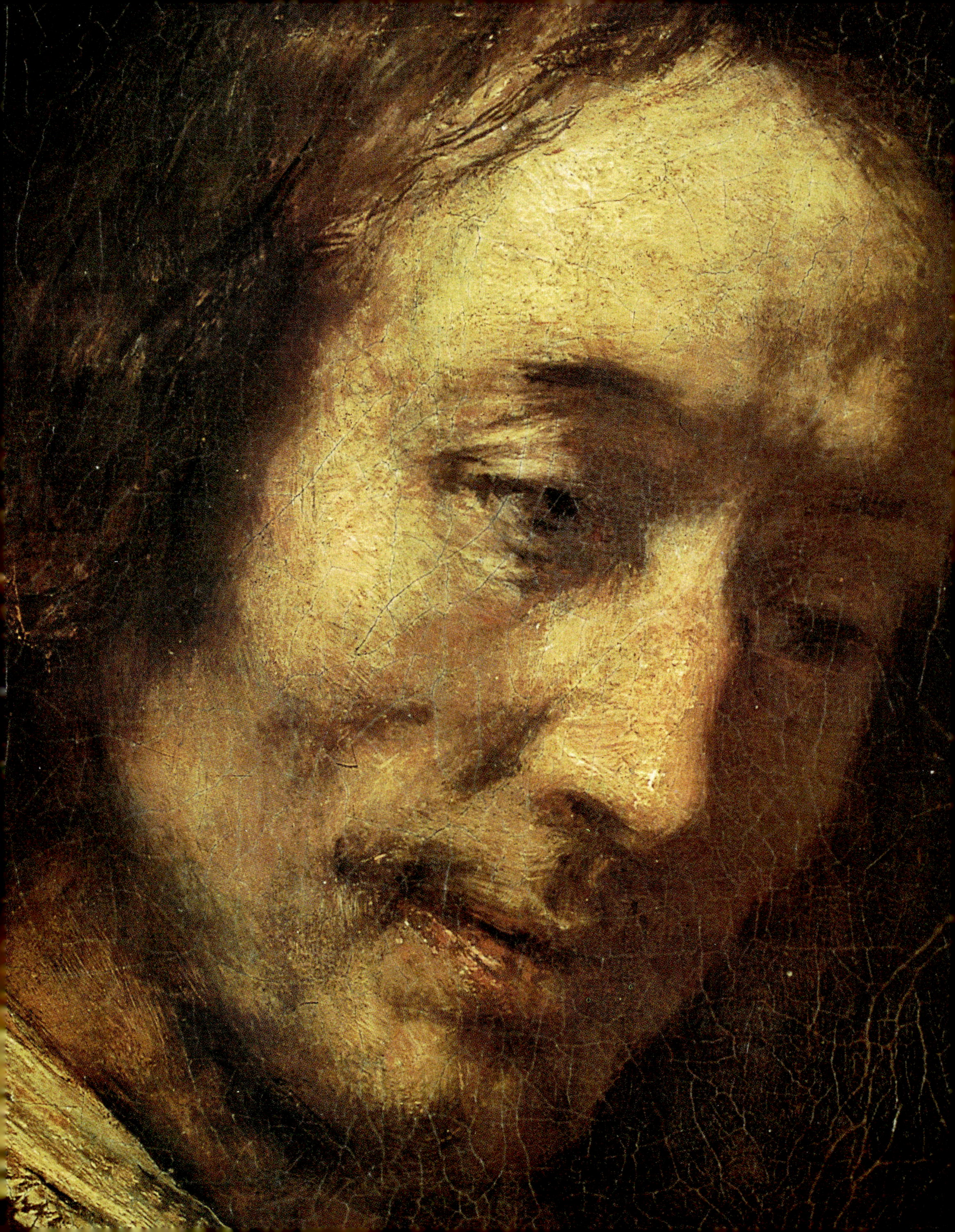

THE GOLDEN AGE

SEVENTEENTH CENTURY FLEMISH (DUTCH) ART, 1588–1672

This period saw the new Dutch Republic (Republic of the Seven United Netherlands) becoming the most powerful maritime and economic powerhouse on earth. North and South Holland (Flanders/Northern Belgium) had the densest population in all Western Europe. Rotterdam was one of the world's largest shipping ports.

The Golden Age was fueled by international trade. This brought wealthy businessmen as patrons of the arts to the Dutch artists of the time, such as Frans Hals, Jan Steen, Jacob van Ruisdael, Hendrick ter Brugghen, Pieter Claesz, Jan Lievens, Gerrit Dow, Pieter de Hooch, Rembrandt van Rijn, and Johannes Vermeer. These artists painted for one thing—money.

Wealthy, middle-class tradesmen and successful mercantile patrons became the driving force fueling commissioned works of art. An explosion of international trade infused the entire area with both power and new wealth. For example, spices like imported nutmeg became so valuable that a bushel of nutmeg was equivalent to the value of a new house. Sadly, toward the end of the seventeenth century, the Franco-Dutch War and the War of the Spanish Succession caused a quick decline for the Golden Age.

It is estimated that for about thirty-years after 1640, approximately 1.3 million Dutch paintings were produced, most of which were portraits commissioned by the large mercantile class. In 1672, France invaded the Dutch Republic. They called it the Rampjaar or "year of disaster." After that, things were never the same. Artists typically went into other lines of work or simply died in poverty. Many artists joined trade associations, such as the Guild of St. Luke, to which Vermeer belonged.

Van Rijn, Rembrandt.
The Jewish Bride (detail). 1665–1669.
Oil on canvas. 47.8 in. x 65.6 in.
Rijksmuseum, Amsterdam, the Netherlands.

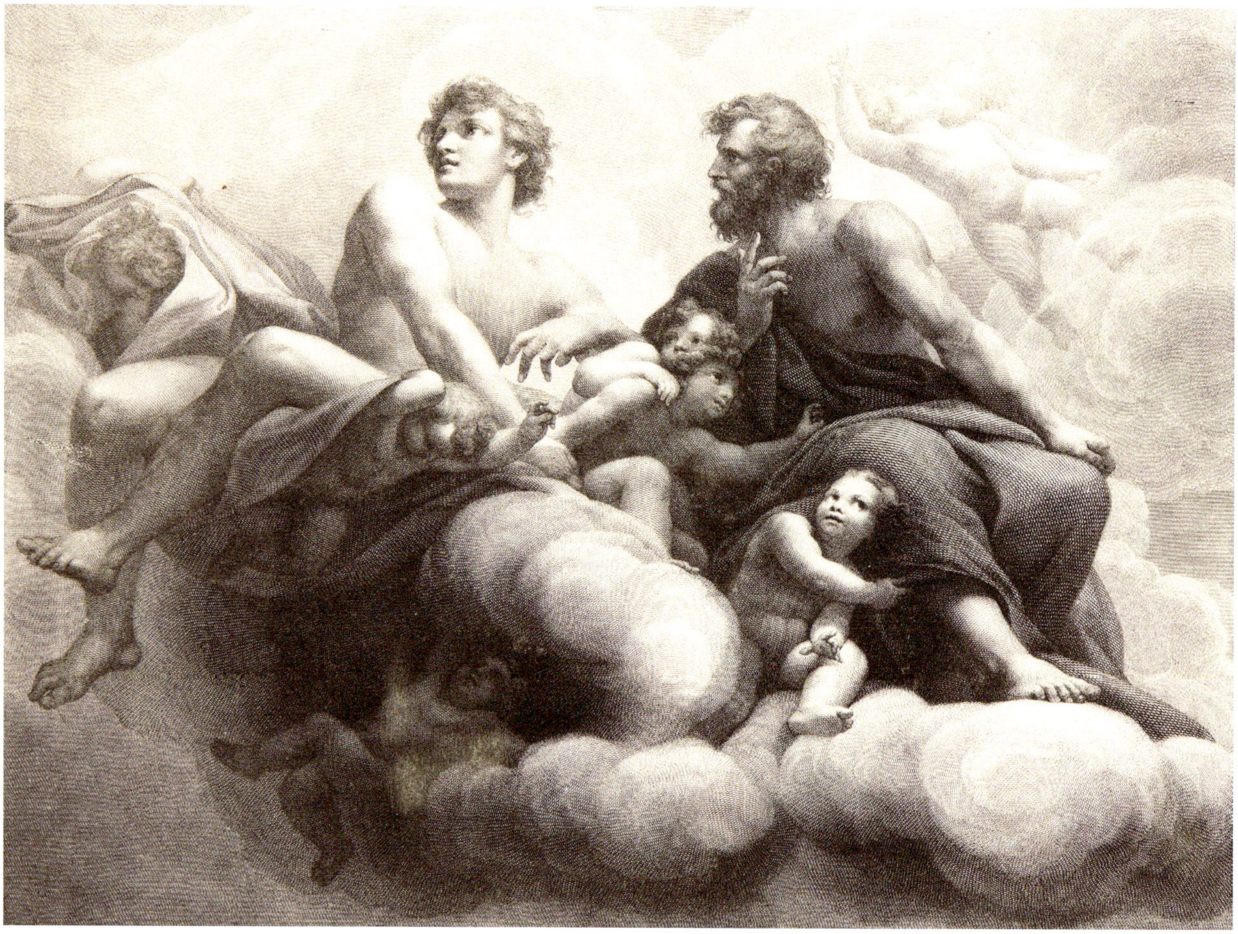

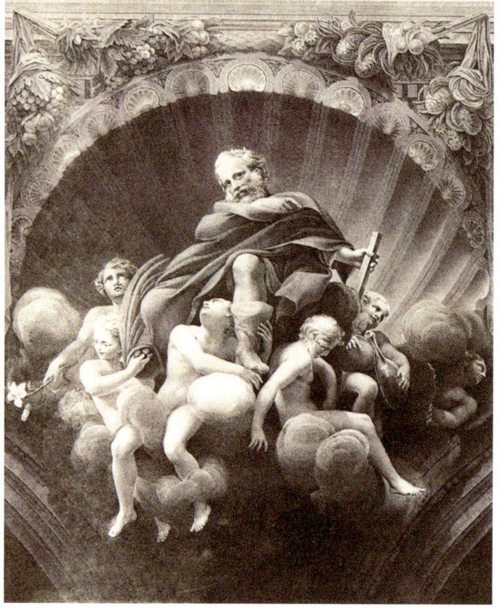

Two Apostles (above). *Saint Thomas* (bottom left).
Engravings by Toschi. The Gray Collection,
Harvard University, Cambridge, Massachusetts.
Original prints from 1875. Author's private collection.

Parmigianino, Francesco.
Lucretia. 1540.
11.75 in. x 8.25 in.
Museo Nazionale di Capodimonte, Naples, Italy.

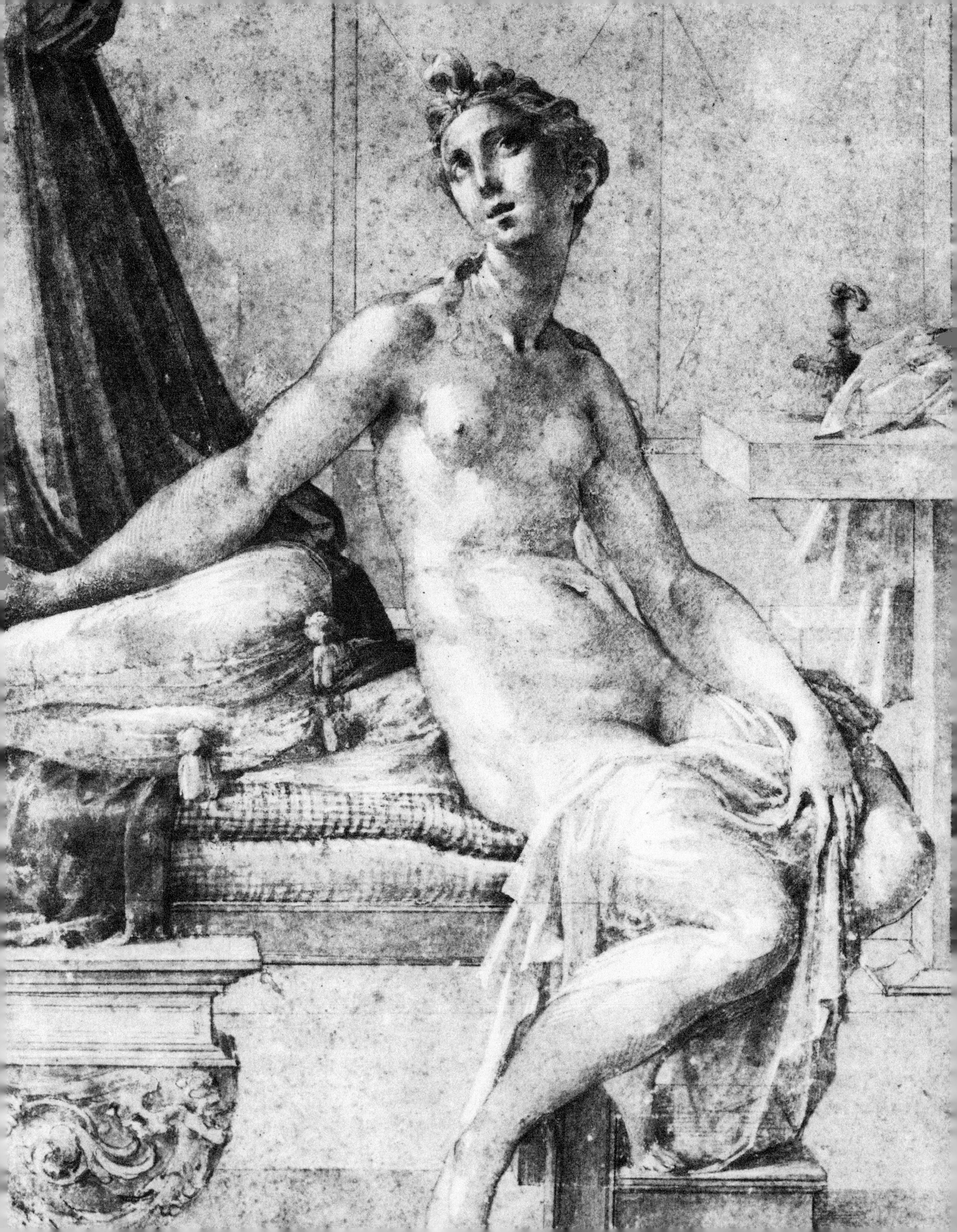

DRAWING—THE CRITICAL FIRST STEP

Museums are filled with the initial drawings of artists prior to their laying down that first stroke of pigmented mixture of linseed oil and turpentine. Often, seeing a drawing of one of the old masters tells more about what they were thinking than the finished product itself, especially once the multiple layers of impastos and glazes have been applied.

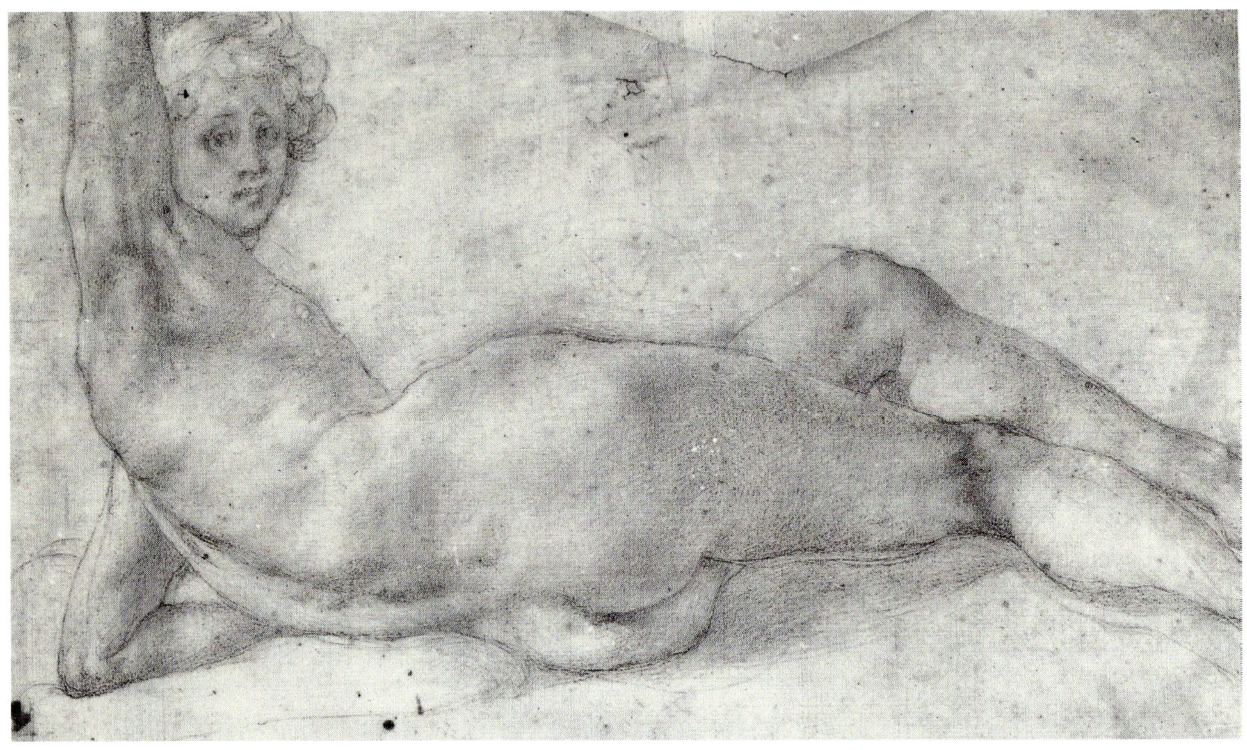

Pontormo, Jacopo Carucci.
Graphite on parchment. 1532. 8.3 in. x 11.4 in.
Cataloged by Carlo Falciani.
Uffizi Gallery, Florence, Italy.

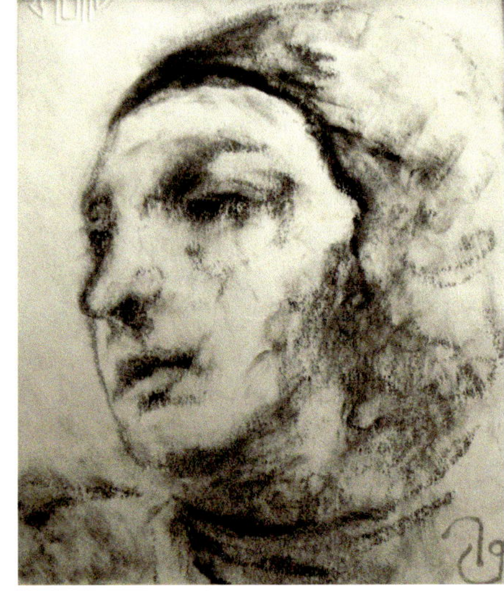

Griffith, Tom. 1983.
Conté crayon on paper. 4 in. x 5 in.
Author's personal collection.

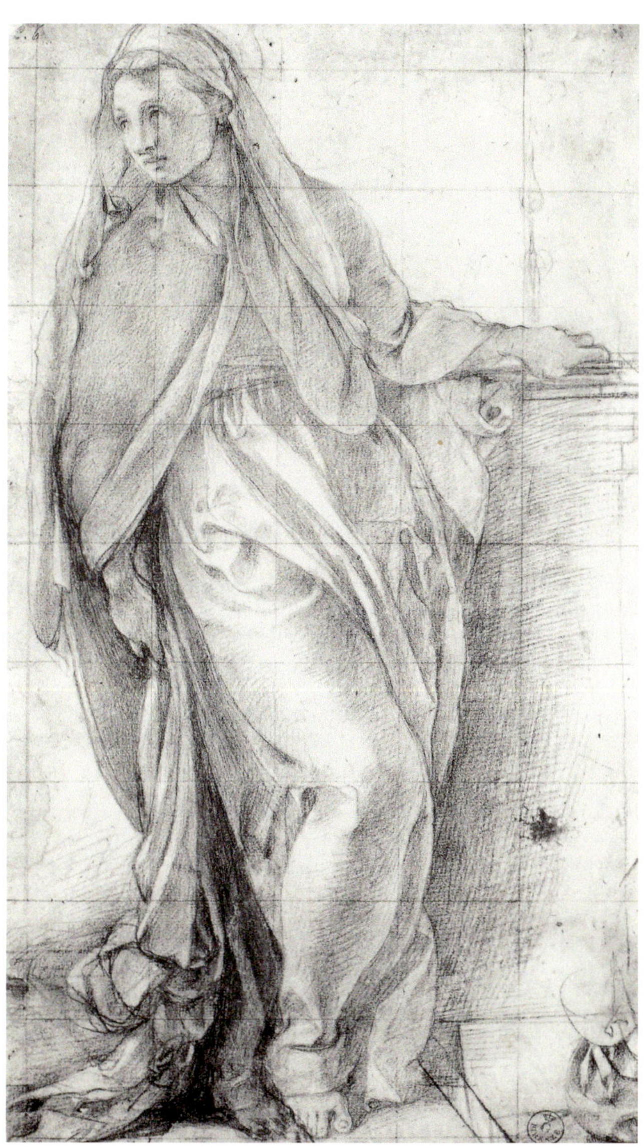

Pontormo, Jacopo Carucci.
Drawing for the *Annunciation*. 1527–1528.
The fresco at St. Felicita, Capponi Chapel.
n. 6653 F. Cataloged by Carlo Falciani.
Uffizi Gallery, Florence, Italy.

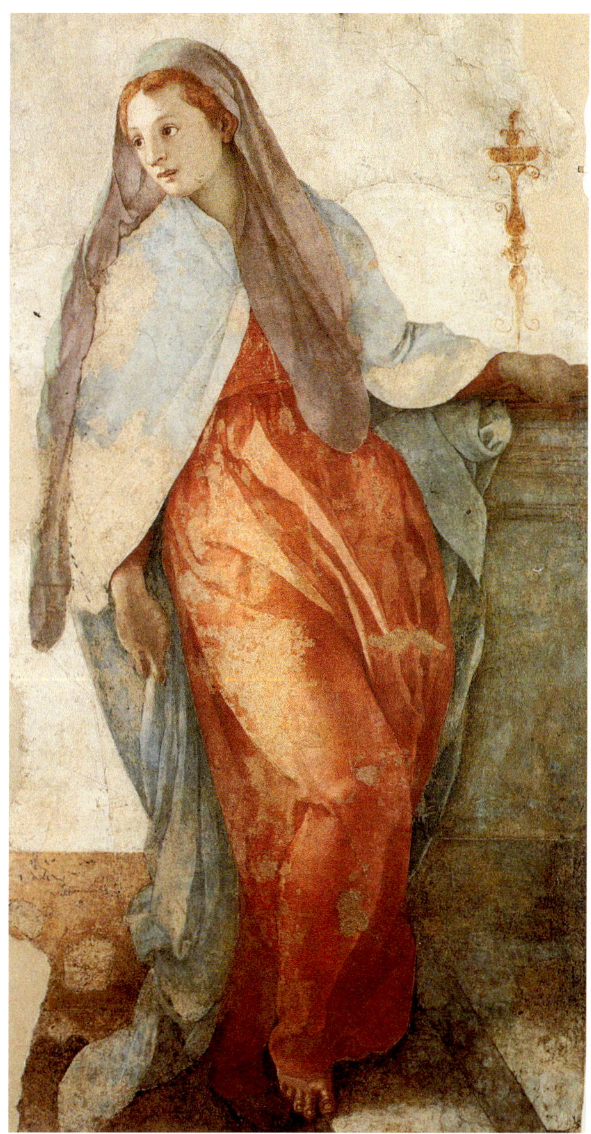

Pontormo, Jacopo Carucci.
Fresco, St. Felicita, Capponi Chapel.
Florence, Italy.

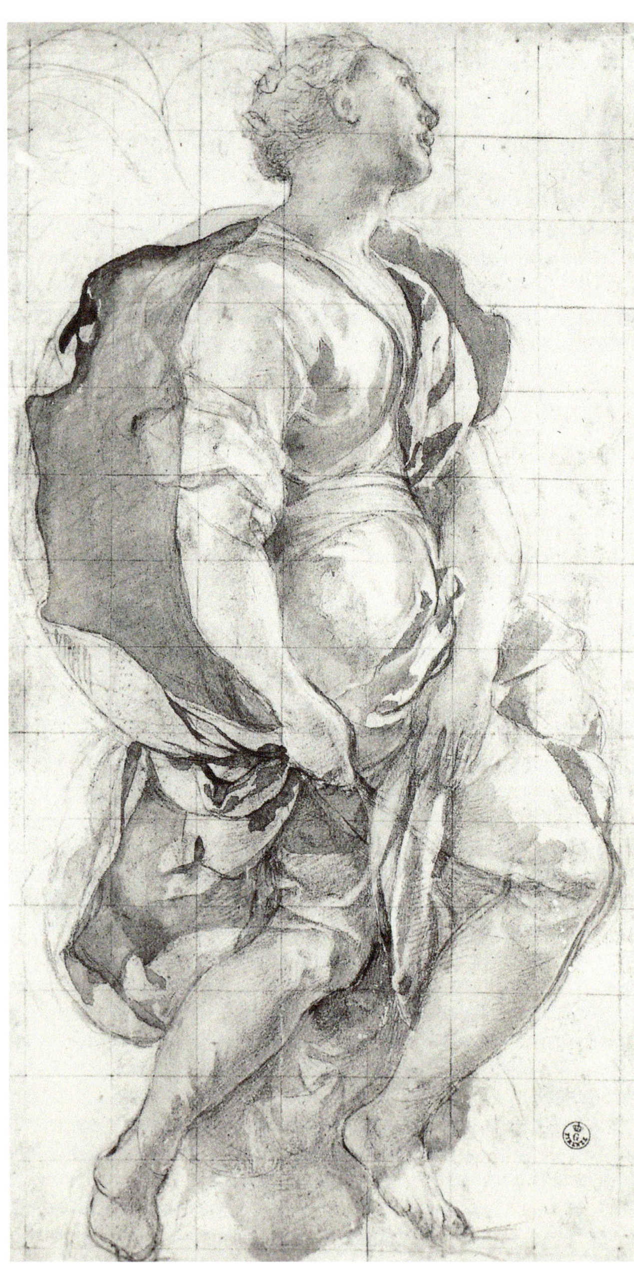

Pontormo, Jacopo Carucci.
Drawing for the *Annunciation*. 1527–1528.
The fresco at St. Felicita, Capponi Chapel.
n. 488 F. Cataloged by Carlo Falciani.
Uffizi Gallery, Florence, Italy.

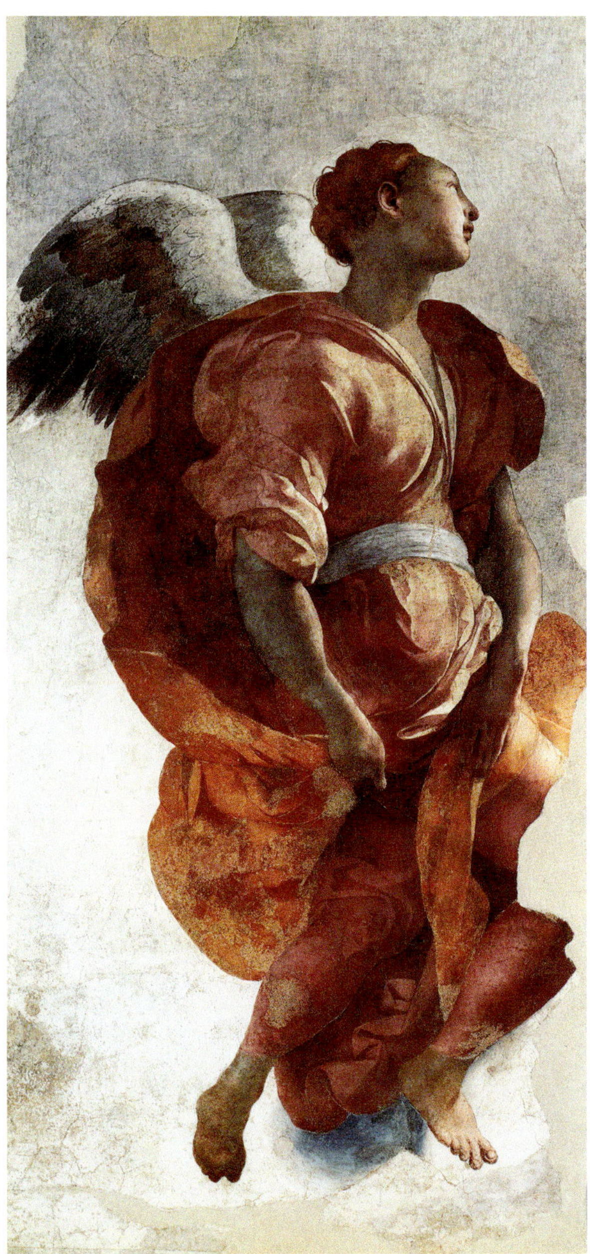

Pontormo, Jacopo Carucci
Fresco, St. Felicita, Capponi Chapel.
Florence, Italy.

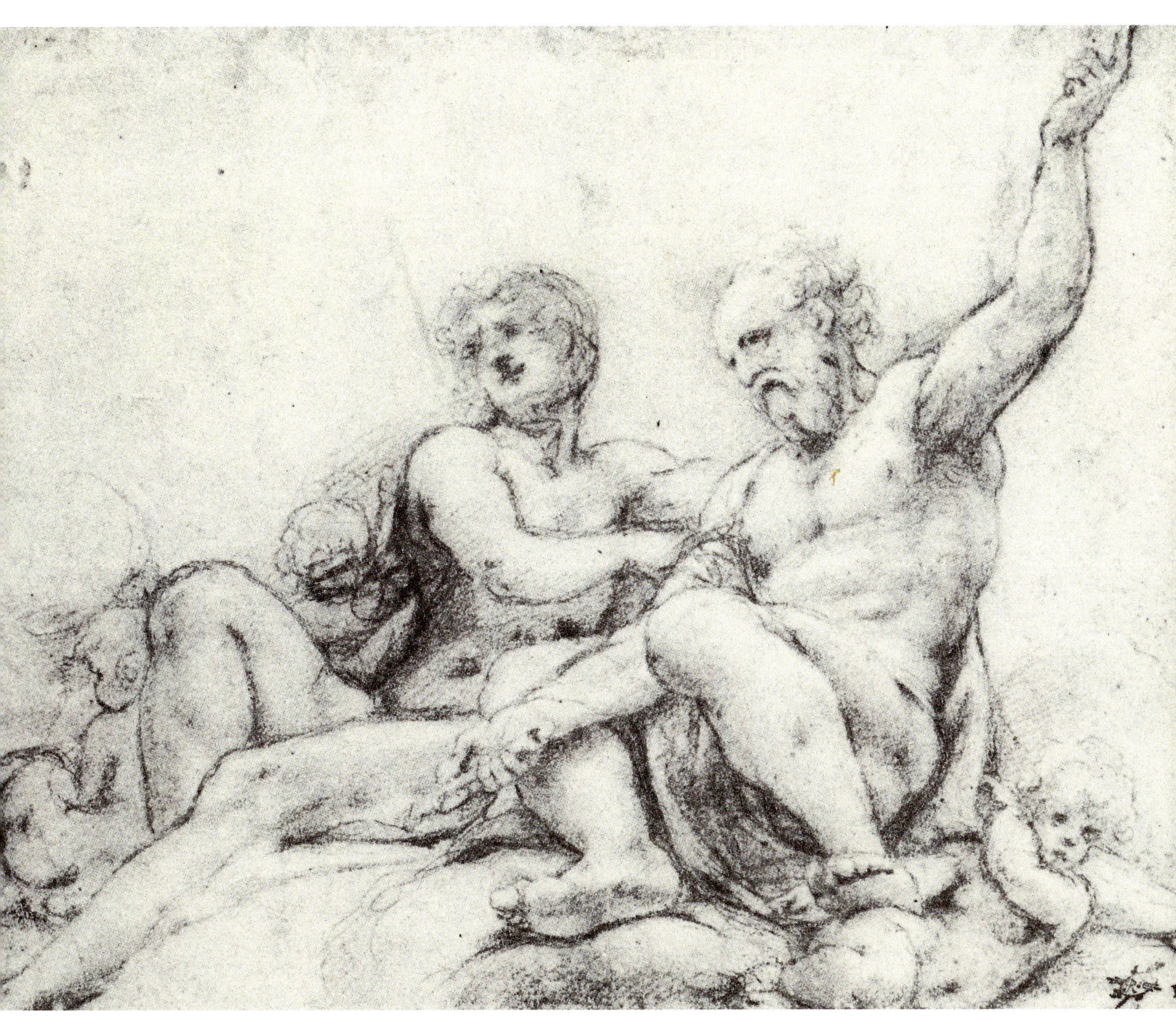

da Correggio, Antonio Allegri
Two Apostles.
Louvre Museum, Paris, France.

FIRST DRAW, THEN PAINT

This book focuses on the face for two reasons. One, as I said before, it is the most difficult thing imaginable to paint. Two, most artists avoid it like the plague. Painting a bowl of fruit or a landscape takes just as much talent as painting a face, but it is the face that gets the most reaction from those who view it.

The *Mona Lisa* by Italian painter Leonardo da Vinci is the most valuable painting in the world. Although time has faded general areas containing certain pigments he used in the painting, her infamous smile is still there! This fact alone is reason enough that I only paint faces.

It has been said in as many art books as I have read over the years that *if one can't draw, one can't paint*. To paint the human face, one absolutely must know how it is constructed and the proportions it possesses. Otherwise, no matter how well one can paint, the face that painter will spend so much time and effort on will not look natural or correct.

Drawing is the key to painting.

da Vinci, Leonardo.
Mona Lisa (detail). 1503.
(Portrait of Lisa Gherardini, Also known as La Gioconda, wife of Francesco del Giocondo).
Oil on wood (poplar). 20.875 in. x 30 in.
Louvre Museum, Paris, France.

Note: The temperature within the bulletproof glass surrounding the *Mona Lisa* is maintained at a constant 43 degrees Fahrenheit. The *Mona Lisa* is owned by the government of France and can never be sold.

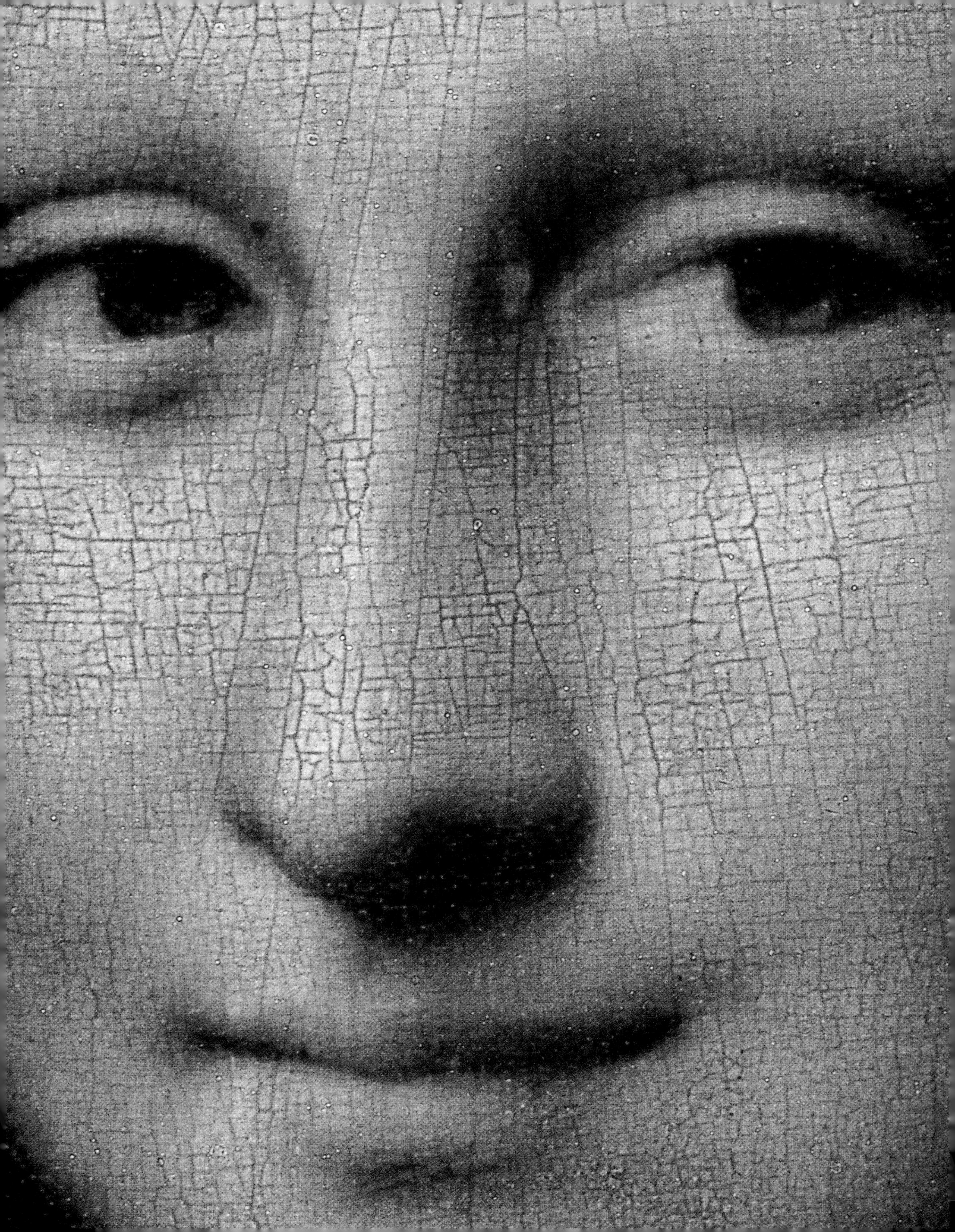

The old masters, and certainly the new ones, would have many drawings in progress at one time. Remember, oil paint takes days, even weeks to dry between applications. Successful artists of the day had staffs of people, including art apprentices, who would build and prepare the canvases, wooden boards, or copper plates in anticipation of the many pieces the artist would be producing. Prior to any actual painting, the artist would draw out the concept they had in mind. Busy artists with many commissioned pieces would basically have an assembly line in place to maximize throughput.

The ability to draw well is not a natural talent, but one that is acquired through practice. Having the ability to draw well comes down to having the talent of perception. Perception is the way your brain translates the size and shape comparison of the many components that make up an object or face in relation to another, then taking that perceived notion and transposing it onto a flat surface such as a wooden panel or canvas.

One of the reasons old drawings and faded sketches are displayed in museums is that the drawing itself turned out so beautifully that it stands alone as a piece of art. Another reason is that the artist died before he could apply paint and finish it. Lastly, some drawings just don't turn out the way the artist had envisioned, and the initial drawing or outline was simply put aside for another day. Sometimes when what is in an artist's head doesn't translate to paper very well, and the idea is scrapped (but not necessarily thrown away). Most artists will admit they have had hundreds of ideas that they will never get to.

da Vinci, Leonardo.
Vitruvian Man.
Brown ink on parchment.

Note: This was one of da Vinci's many attempts to pen his own thoughts on the proportions of the human head and the accompanying facial features.

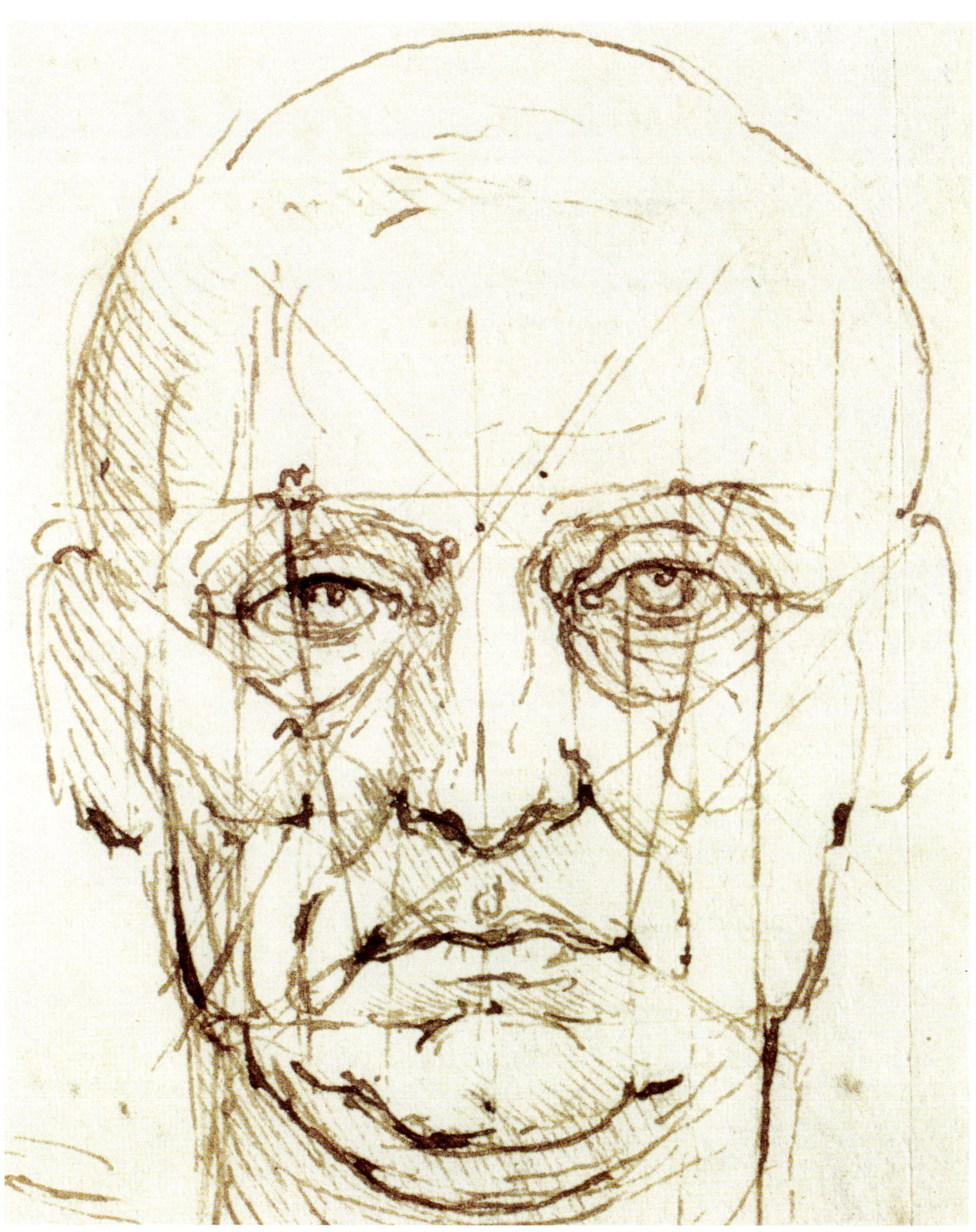

In painting the face, knowing the bone and muscular structure of that face is critical. Drawing is a wonderful way to lay it all out prior to starting with the actual paint. Plus, the drawing serves as a preview as to whether the artist's vision is going to work.

Once drawn out, the initial sketch can also indicate whether there is too much going on in the piece or not enough. I have seen many preserved drawings of the old masters that later became a finished, painted piece where some of the elements in the drawing didn't make the final cut by the time the painting was completed, framed, and hung on the wall. On the other hand, many an object, face, facial expression, body position, or hand gesture drawn for one painting can end up in another.

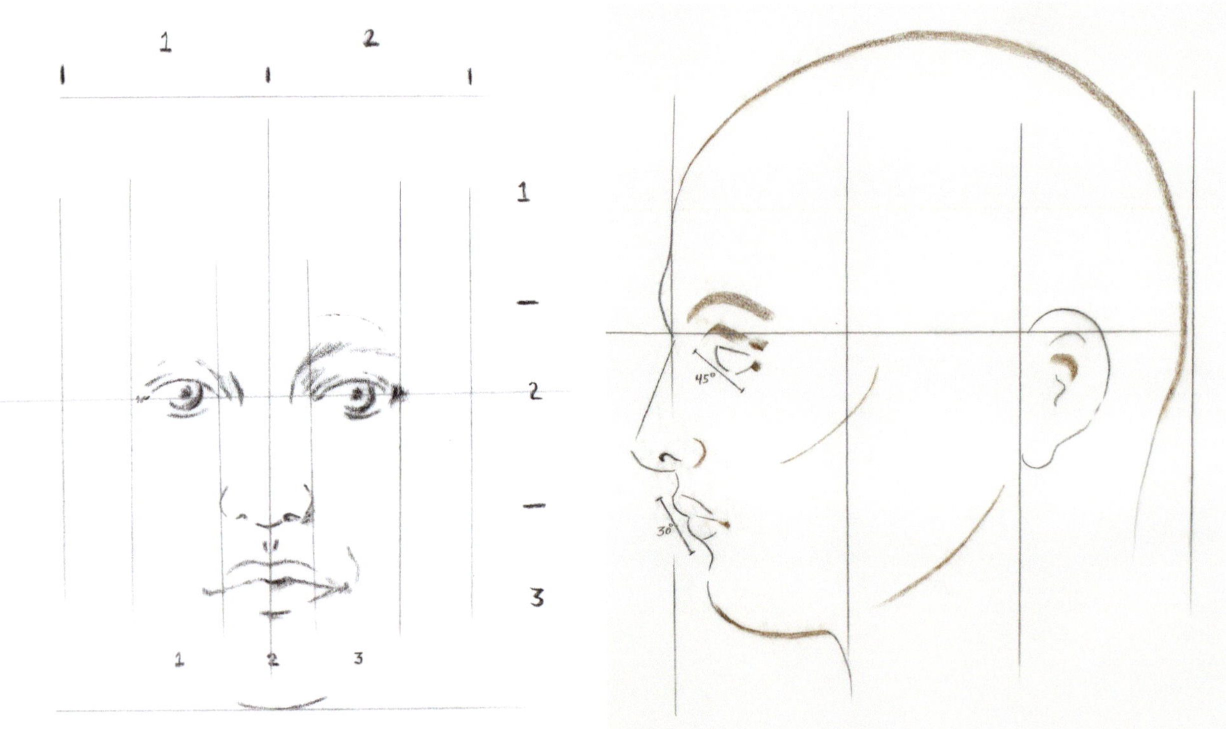

PROPORTIONS OF THE HUMAN FACE THE GOLDEN RATIO

There have been countless studies done on the ideal proportions of the human face for others to interpret as an ideal attractive face. The relationship between the height and width of the human face is referred to as the *Golden Ratio*.

In about 500 B.C., the Greeks were believed to be the first to conclude that the 1 (short side) by 1.618 (long side) ratio presented itself as an appealing proportion.

Example: If the width of a face you are painting is 5 inches wide, the height of that face would be 5 x 1.618, or 8.09 inches.

OBSERVATION

I have noticed over the years that the most well-known faces ever painted generally seem to fall within a certain range when it comes to size—between the parameters of 5 to 7 inches wide and 6 to 9 inches tall. Furthermore, the size of the canvas, board, or copper plate they were painted on was relatively small.

The following are examples of the size of a few notable paintings. Keep in mind that the faces on these pieces are much smaller.

- Vermeer's *Girl with the Red Hat* and *Girl with the Pearl Earring* are just 7 in. x 9 in.
- Van Eyck's *Man in the Red Turban* is only 7.5 in. x 10 in.
- da Vinci's *Mona Lisa* is 21 in. x 30 in., but her face is only about 4.5 in. wide and 6 in. tall. That one-inch smile is worth approximately $1 billion.
- *Whistler's Mother* is 64 in. x 57 in., yet the focal point, her face, is a mere 4.5 in. x 6.75 in.

Lastly, the painting I did for the cover of this book is 9 in. x 11 in. The face itself is 4.5 in. x 6 in. I have unconsciously used this size on at least a dozen of my paintings. It wasn't until recently that I realized that this is the most comfortable size to paint a face. Like in Vermeer's work, the panel size of 7 in. x 9 in. seems to be most comfortable and fitting.

I have thrown the painting on page 51 away three times over the last thirty years. But each time I dug it out of the trash and stuck it back in storage. I painted this face from a book I picked up depicting images from the Holocaust. The image on the woman's face was so distraught, I felt I had to paint it. Unfortunately, I got carried away sanding off some of the glaze coats to the point the electric sander went through the layers of impasto and right down to the wooden panel.

In preparation for this book, I decided I would try to repair that Holocaust painting. Two-thirds of the nose was gone, and the entire lower right was badly marred. After thirty years, it was just a guess how I originally painted it. I felt it important to do so because this painting represented one of the first pieces I did on a larger scale (12 in. x 16 in.).

More importantly, for the first time, I used an electric DA (dual action orbital) sander, and it was a reminder not to push too hard! There were thirty glaze coats of olive green and alizarin crimson over the top of the whites and skin tones. The sander took off pretty much all of them, except where the dark glazes crept into only the heaviest brushstrokes in the layers of impasto.

This technique of aging a painting cannot be achieved merely with a brush and scrapper. The sander leaves the painted panel glass smooth. This is yet another reason to use wooden panels. This aging (adding patina) method of finishing work could never be accomplished by painting on canvas.

Griffith, Tom.
Survivor. 1992. Oil on wood. 12 in. x 16 in.
Author's personal collection.

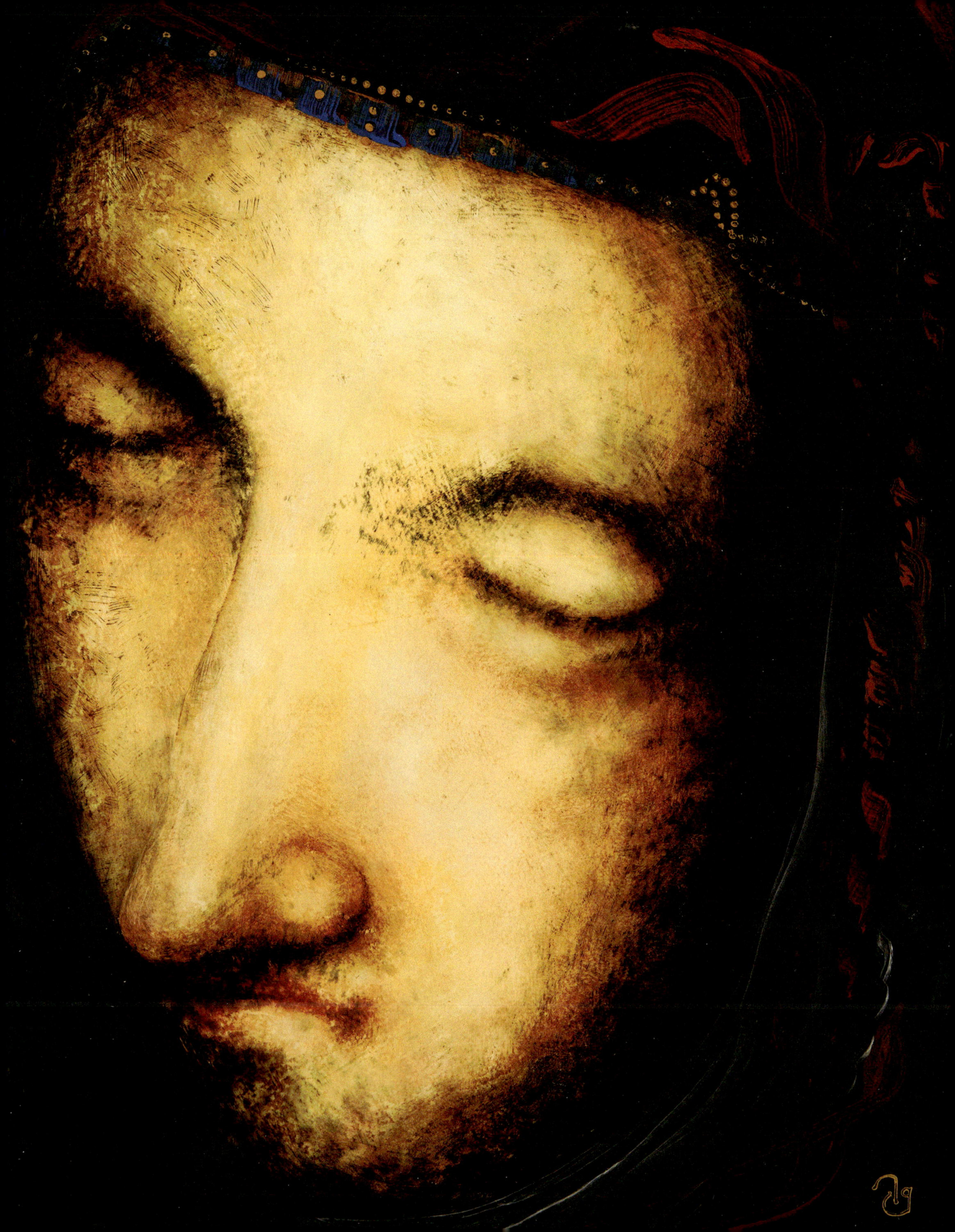

THE HUMAN FACE

What colors make up the perfect flesh tone? Well, it depends on many factors, including the race of your subject.

Other than those races with very dark skin, most faces can be painted with basically three or four colors and then toned to the appropriate shade.

It is generally believed that the old masters used yellow ochre, vermilion and/or burnt sienna plus white to create white European skin tones.

Rembrandt never worked on a white surface. Rather he always started with what is called a "ground." In his case, the ground was mixed with earth tones plus a grayish brown. The gray was made by mixing black and white into the earth tones of natural earth pigments using the umbers (umbra) and siennas.

Commentary: Throughout this book, two words keep coming up: impasto and glazes. If nothing else is taken from these pages, please just remember one thing:

If there is any one key to realism in attempting to capture the human face, it is the extensive use of layers of paint and semi-transparent and transparent glazes for the light to both pass through and reflect from. The sum total of these factors provides a luminescence that simply cannot be achieved with even the most carefully thought-out stroke of a single color loaded on the tip of a brush.

Rule of thumb: Detail that cannot be seen in a photo does not belong in the painting either. This specifically goes for eyelashes, individual eyebrow hairs, creases around the mouth, etc. The best faces I have ever seen only demonstrate that less is more. Letting the brushstrokes and use of color and shadows do the work ensures the painter will never need that tiny, pointed brush bought at the art store.

The digitized detail of one of Caravaggio's most notable paintings (right) demonstrates how many colors the human eye is really seeing.

After many years of personal research and visits to art museums around the world, as well as experimentation with endless "magic mixtures" of colors, I have narrowed it down to what works best for me.

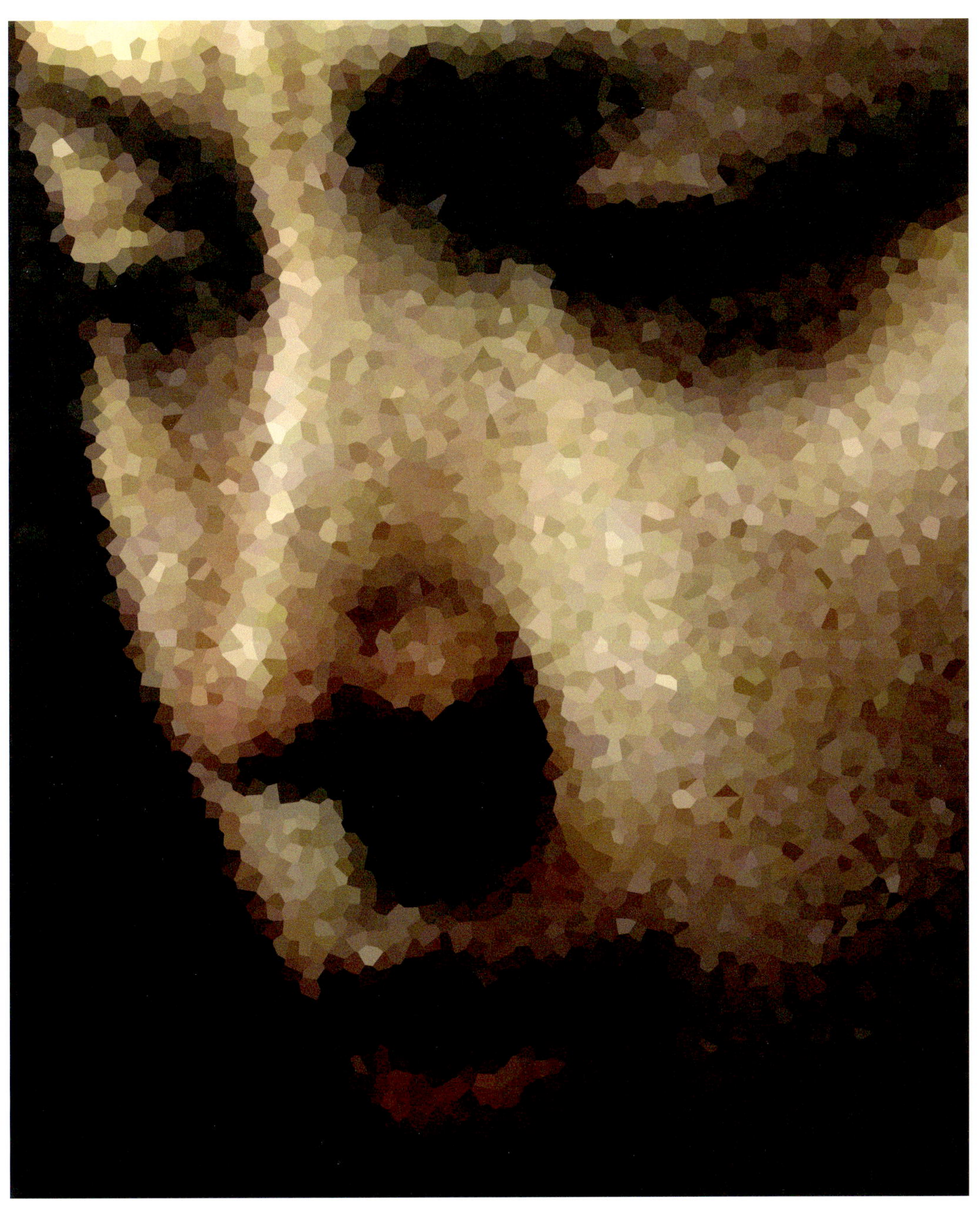

Caravaggio, Michelangelo Merisi.
Judith Beheading Holofernes (detail). 1598–1602.
Oil on canvas. 77 in. x 57 in.
Galleria Nazionale d'Arte, Palazzo Barberini.
Rome, Italy.
Digitally altered.

THE MAGIC FOUR

Titanium white • Naples yellow • Alizarin crimson • Olive green

These four colors are merely my choice of colors. That is not to say that they are the right ones, because there are no right ones.

Tonal value colors: titanium white, Naples yellow, and alizarin crimson.

Shadows and darker-skinned races: alizarin crimson and olive green, and sometimes a little Prussian blue and/or burnt umber or Van Dyke brown.

Skin tone options for white European faces. Note: for African and darker-skinned races, ignore the "Whites" column on the left and use the last three columns with special focus on the raw and burnt umber, as well as Van Dyck brown.

Whites	**Yellows**	**Reds**	**Shadows (Blues, Greens, & Browns)**
Lead white	Lead-tin yellow	Venetian red	Prussian blue
Zinc white	Naples yellow	Alizarin crimson*	Azurite
Titanium white	Yellow ochre	Vermilion	Olive green
Flake white	Raw sienna	Madder lake	Verdigris
	Cadmium yellow	Cadmium red	Phthalo green
		Red ochre	Earth green
		Carmine lake	Ultramarine
			Raw or burnt umber
			Smalt
			Phthalo blue
			Cobalt blue
			French ultramarine
			Chromium oxide
			Van Dyke brown

*Alizarin crimson has been proven to fade over time. The only one I have found that does not, is made by Gamblin (called Alizarin Permanent). I personally use Gamblin FastMatte (alkyd).

The most successful portraiture one can paint involves a heavily textured undercoat (impasto), topped with multiple thin, transparent layers of tinted glaze. However, not all of the great masters utilized the same methods of achieving what they thought was the optimal goal of chiaroscuro (light and dark). Michelangelo took it one step further by "scraping off" some of the glaze coats to expose the lead white underbase below, resulting in an even more dramatic highlighted area.

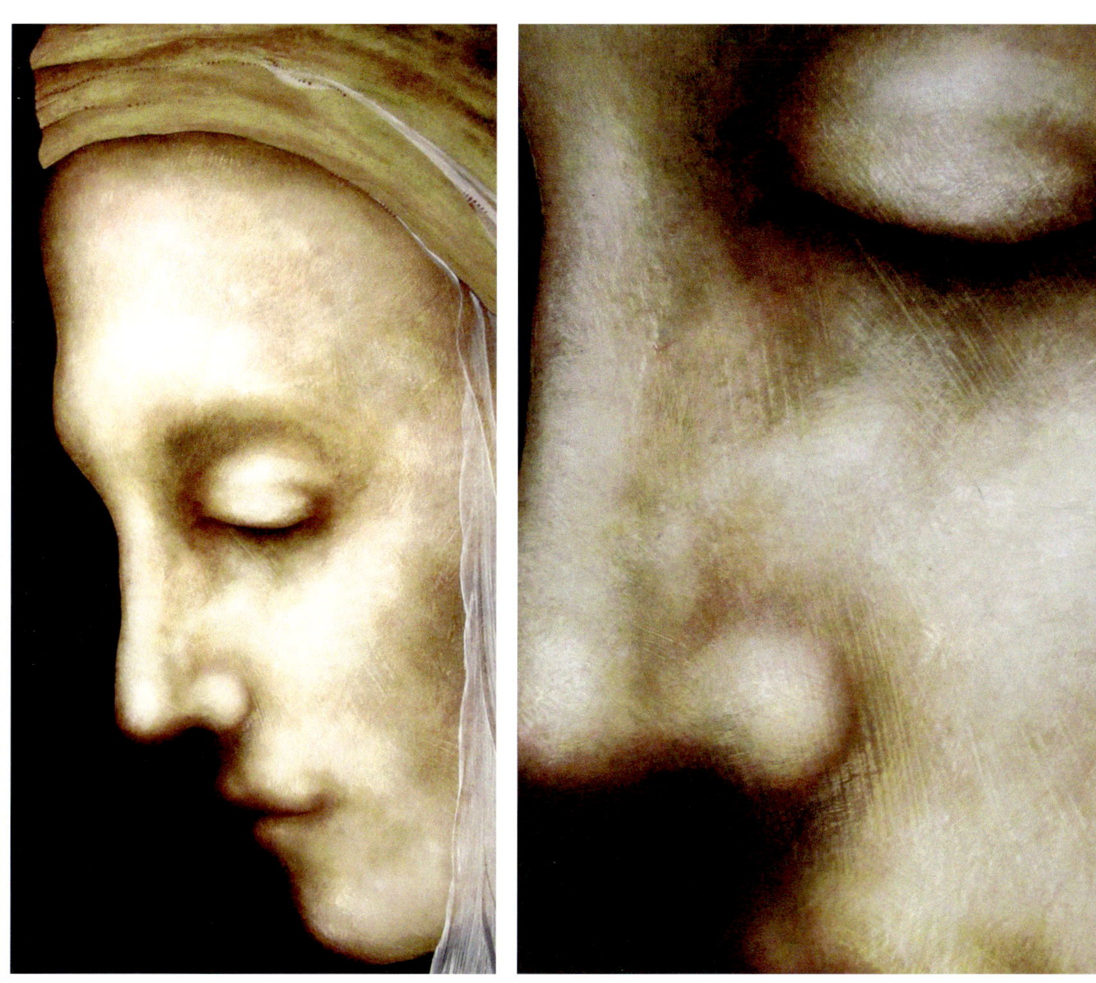

Griffith, Tom.
2004. Oil on wood. 17.5 in. x 39.5 in.
Author's personal collection.

There are many manufacturers of oil paint. The color stamped on the label varies greatly from one maker to the next. In fact, sometimes with the cheaper brands, the color doesn't come close to what is labeled. Go with quality. This is one category of products that it really matters. When it comes to choosing a pigmented oil paint, you get what you pay for.

Most great artists worked with a very limited selection of colors on their palette. It isn't necessary to purchase fifty colors of oil paints to arrive at the end goal. Plus, a limited palette forces an artist to mix subtle and sometimes not so subtle variations of the colors available while learning something at the same time.

Caution: When using blue as a shadow-added color, reds and blues can result in various shades of purple.

Progression of paint layers going from light to dark using generic colors:

Highlight (Impasto)	**Peach Tone**	**Shadow/Skin Tone**	**Dark Shadow/Skin Tone**
white	white	red + green	red + green
	yellow + red	or + blue	or + dark blue
		and/or	and/or
		burnt umbers	burnt umbers
			and very dark browns

Keep in mind that in terms of the dark shadow, mixing red, green, and blue makes black. Sometimes this is what the painter wants without having to use actual black out of the tube. There is a difference.

SHADOWS

Neutral shadows: burnt sienna and ultramarine

Warm shadows: cadmium red or permanent rose with ultramarine and burnt sienna

Cool shadows: ultramarine or phthalo blue and burnt sienna (Note: Replace burnt sienna with burnt umber for extra depth.)

Very deep shadows: phthalo blue and burnt umber (Note: Add permanent rose or alizarin crimson for extra deep shadows.)

THE SHADOW FORMULA

The general rule for painting shadows is that the shadow of any color includes the color(s) of the object or face mixed with its complementary color and possibly a touch of blue. Example: a red apple's shadow is its tonal color (red) mixed with its complementary (opposite) color, green, and a touch of blue.

Hint: Add a touch of blue to any shadow. There have been many studies performed on the actual color of shadows. Since the factor of light plays into the tonal color of everything, it has been shown that blue is present in almost every shadow. It all has to do with the spectrum of light and other factors in nature that are simply too complex to explain here.

To find a color's complementary (opposite) color for creating shadows, use a color wheel.

Warning: The complement of light yellow is violet (purple), whereas the complement of medium yellow is blue. Also, the complement of red is green, but the complement of light green is a mix of red and violet. Check the color wheel. Learning how to use the color wheel to create shadows is often the difference between a good painting and a great painting.

Note: The color of a shadow also contains the other colors in the area reflecting off the object for which the shadow is being created. However, getting too involved in adding those other surrounding colors can result in mud. When mud is accidentally created as a color, it is hard to reverse it by adding even more colors.

WHAT SURFACE SHOULD I PAINT ON?

Basically, there are two choices when deciding which surface to paint on: stretched canvas or wooden panels. I have always used wood panels for the following reasons: First, I tend to buy old frames and mirrors in which to place my finished pieces. Most are well over a hundred years old, and the sizes never seem to be the standard 8 inches x 10 inches or 16 inches x 20 inches. Therefore, wood comes in quite handy because it can be cut to the exact size desired. Plus, what if the coolest 150-year-old Eastlake mirror is seven feet tall and is wider at the top than it is at the bottom? The frame itself can inspire me to paint something to put in it.

Second, and more importantly, let's say I paint something that is exquisite, and I want it to be around for hundreds of years after I'm gone. Which is most likely still to be there? A painting on canvas that can get torn, water-damaged, or mold-ridden from improper storage? Or a half-inch-thick piece of wood? I believe in a sturdy wooden panel that can be thrown against the wall and barely dented. Something to think about.

Types of Wood Typically Used During the Golden Age

Italy: white poplar

Flanders/Flemish (Northern Belgium/the Netherlands): oak

Spain: oak, cedar, walnut, beech, chestnut, and cedar

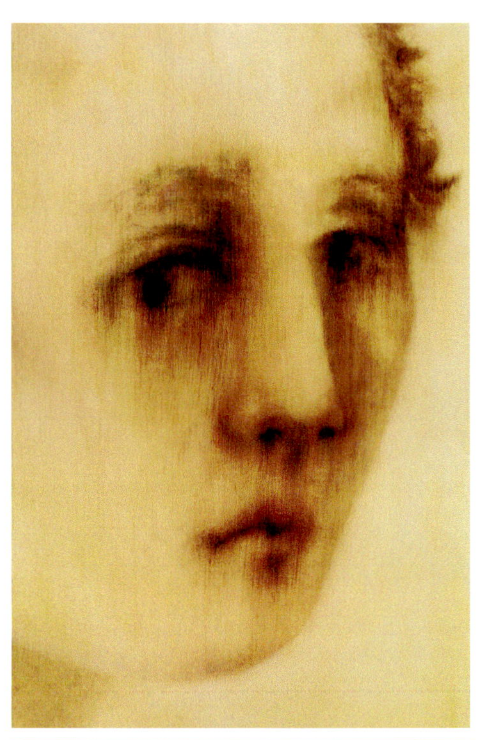

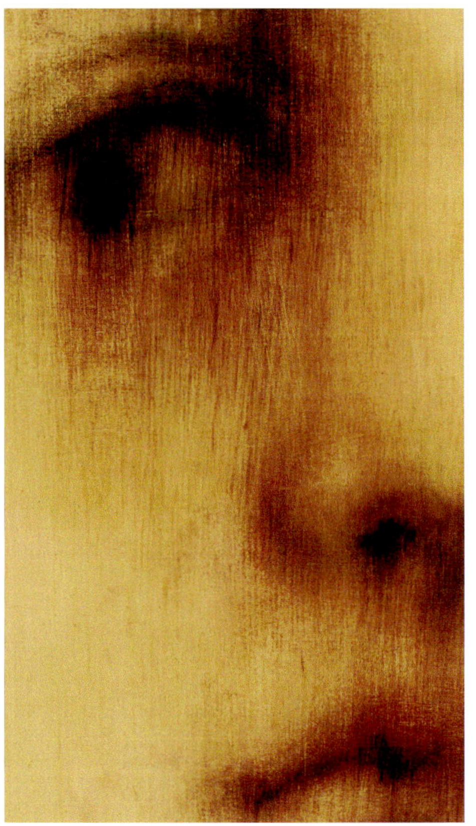

Griffith, Tom,
2011. Oil on wood. 8 in. x 10 in.
Tan gesso board with two colors:
alizarin crimson and olive green.
Author's personal collection.

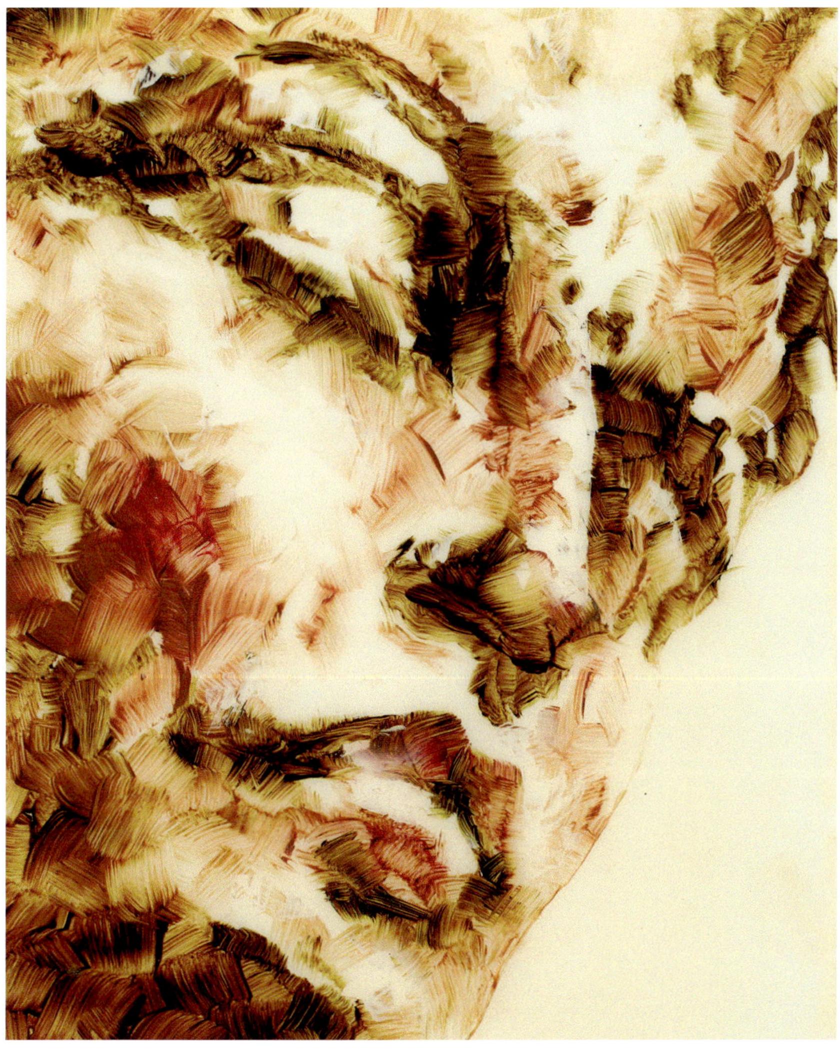

Griffith, Tom.
2000. Oil on wood.
17.5 in x 19.5 in.
Author's personal collection.

This oil painting reflects everything needed to know about painting the human face. The preliminary underpainting using only olive green and alizarin crimson forms the basis of the painting. Normally after this step, the heavy, highly textured impasto using titanium white and Naples yellow would be applied. In this case, however, it was left as is as a demonstration piece to visitors of how a painting starts out.

Note: The most important brushstrokes of this painting—and any other face for that matter—are the shadows formed under the tip of the nose just above the nostrils. Always start with the nose when painting a face. Why? Because if the nose doesn't turn out, neither will the rest of the face. The shadow above the nostril is the hardest part of any face to paint.

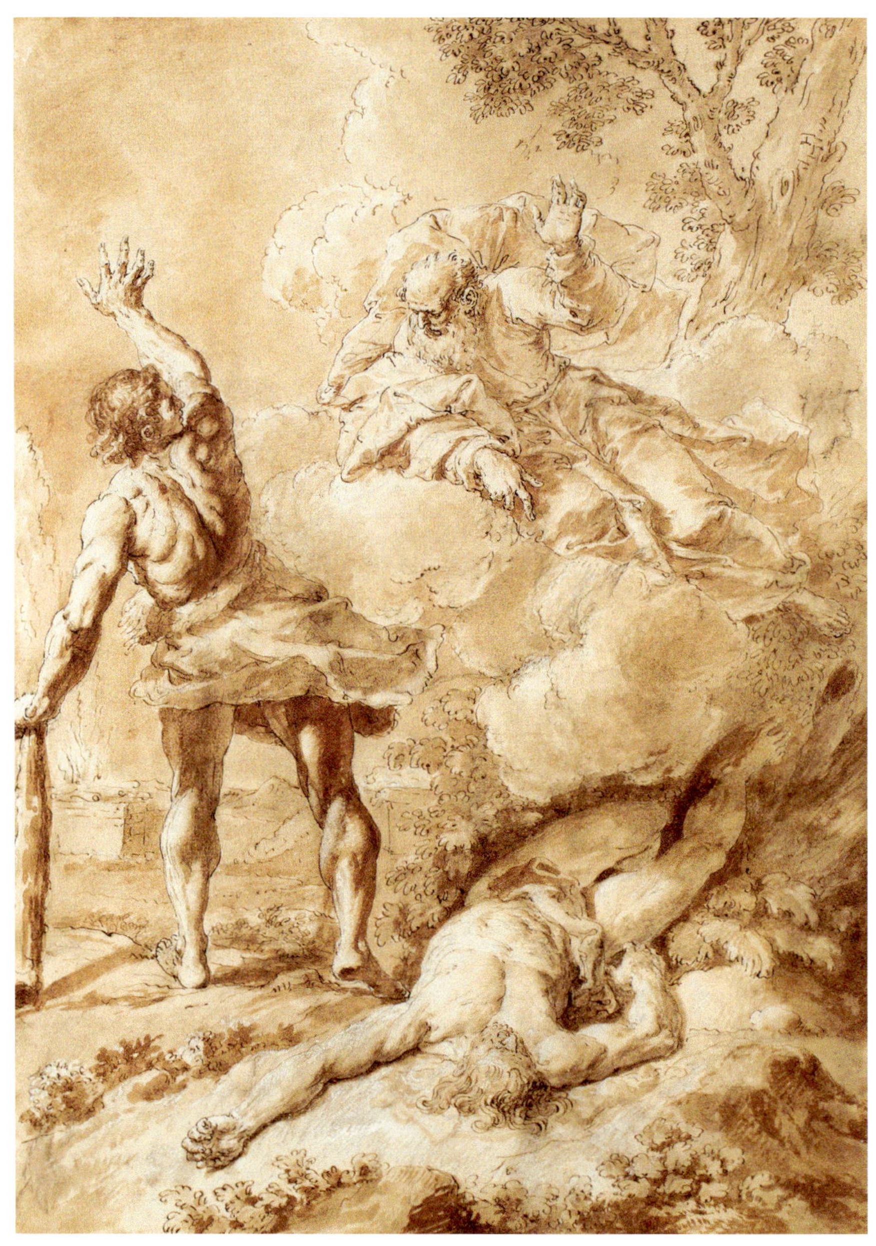

Fontebasso, Francesco.
God confronting Cain after he slew Able.
Pen and brown ink, brownish wash, and black chalk. 12.5 in. x 17.9 in.

Note: This represents one step beyond the drawing. The brownish wash coat applied here indicates to the artist where the lightened and shadowed areas are to fall once the painting begins. The wash coat also indicates how the painting is going to look as the artist envisioned.

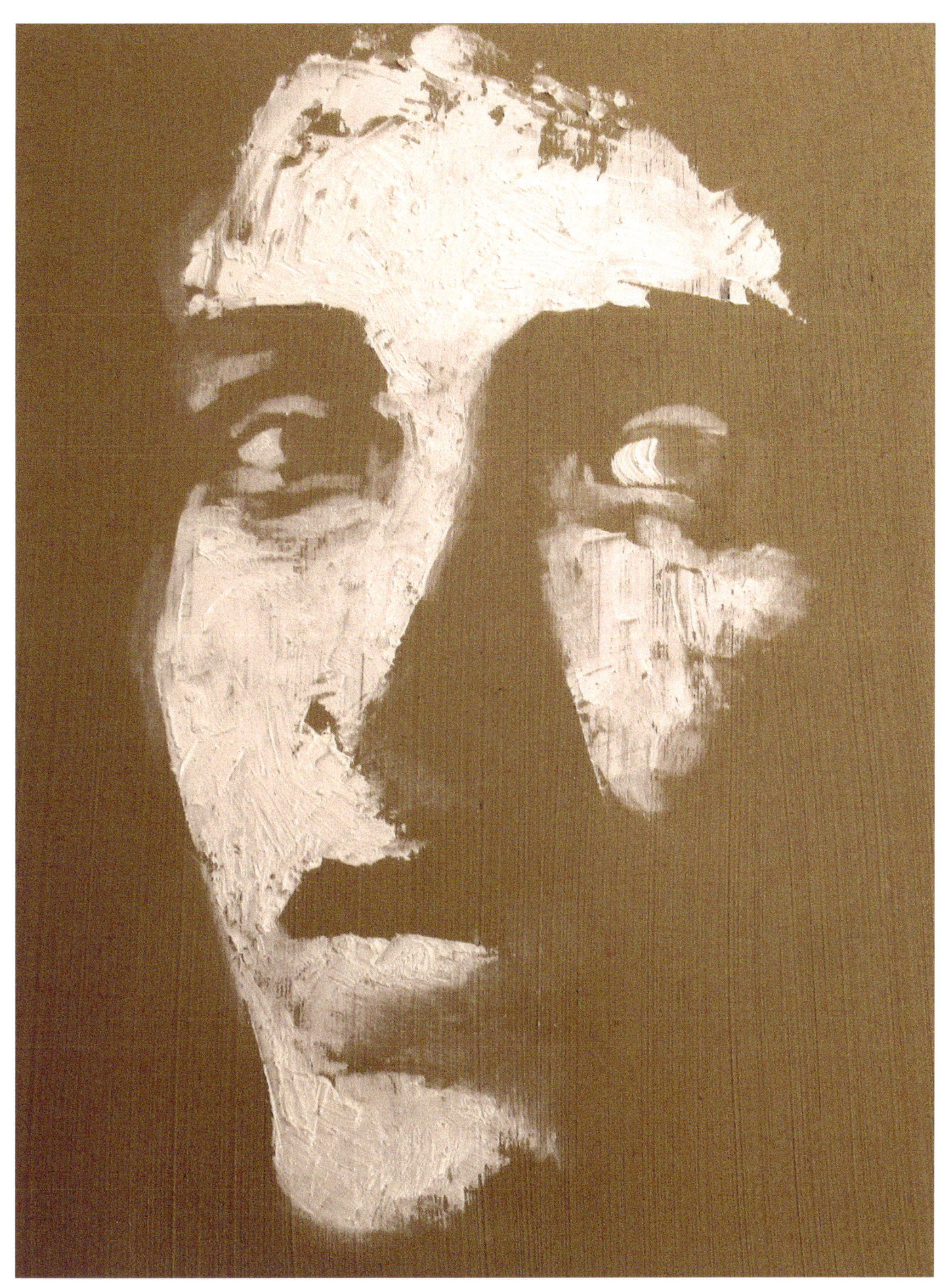

Griffith, Tom.
2021. Oil on wood. 7 in. x 9 in.
Author's personal collection.

GETTING STARTED

BLOCKING (ALSO REFERRED TO AS THE BLOCK-IN)

Blocking is a method of preparing the surface to be painted by using a transparent tinted wash, usually consisting of tones of brown, to indicate what goes where. This critical step assures the artist that what they have in their head translates to the canvas or board. The initial blocking lays out the general sizes and placement of the subject to be painted. Blocking is basically a mind's test run. I have blocked countless boards, only to change my mind and go to plan B. What is in the painter's head doesn't always translate well to the board. As best put by artist Richard Schmid, block-in is like "...sneaking up on the subject in one way or another."

UNDERPAINTING

Underpainting is the base of the face to be painted. Underpainting is really the first layer of paint laid down normally using very light colors indicating where the highlights will be. This underpaint is often white or off-white, thick, and textured. This step generally can indicate whether what is intended actually looks proportionally correct from the start.

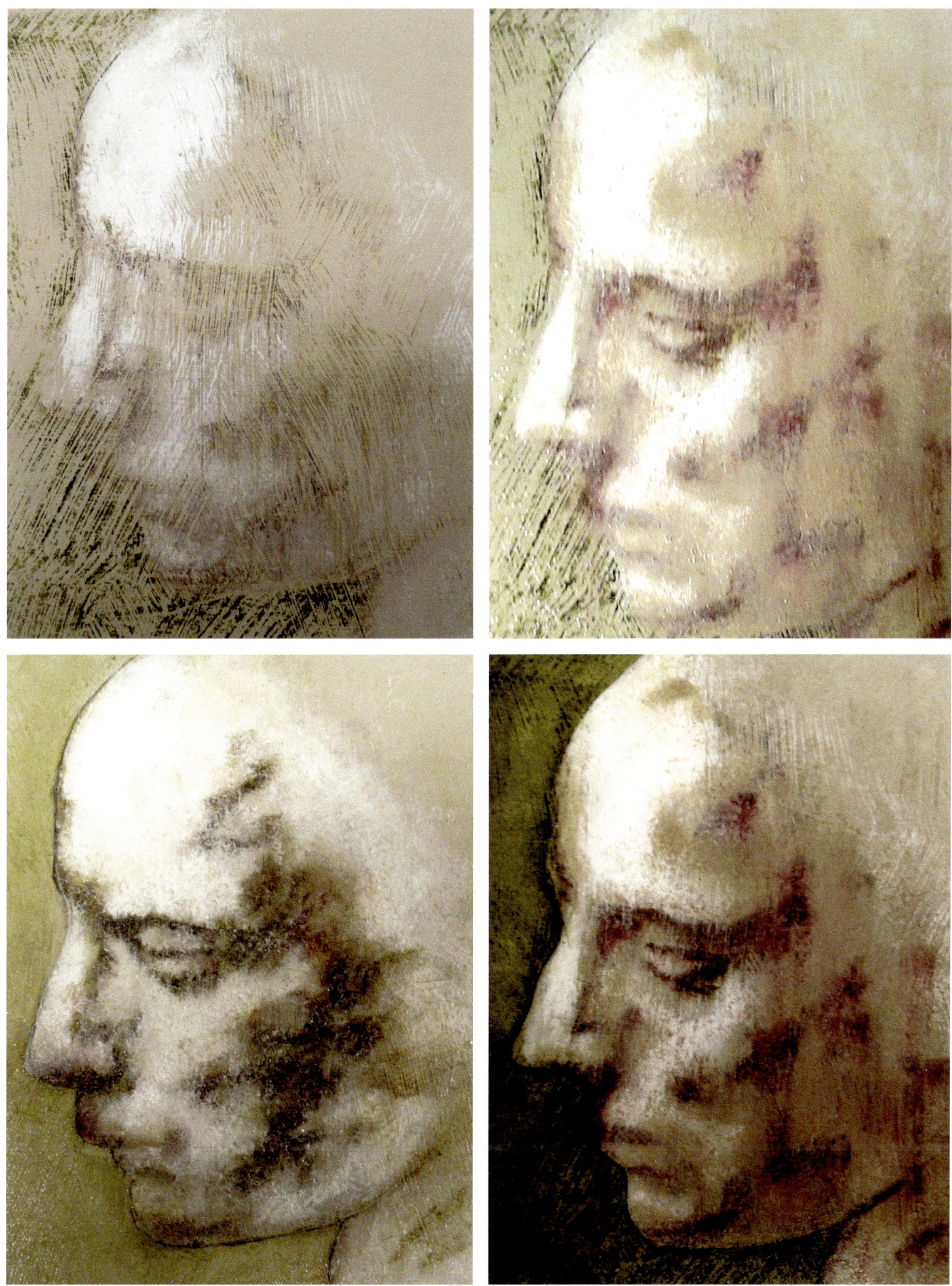

LESS IS MORE

A statement that was never truer, especially when it comes to art.

Trying to put too much detail into a painting can, and usually does, ruin a painting. Many artists spend countless hours on detail, all the while making the painting worse. Look closely at some of the greatest works of art throughout the ages. Many aspects of these masterpieces have mere suggestions of an object, building, or landscape in the background, turning all the focus onto the main subject. Plus, why spend all that time on surrounding objects, merely distracting the viewer from what the artist really wants them to see?

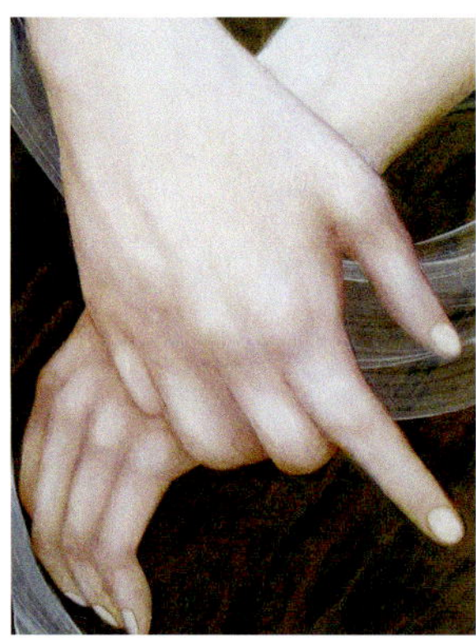

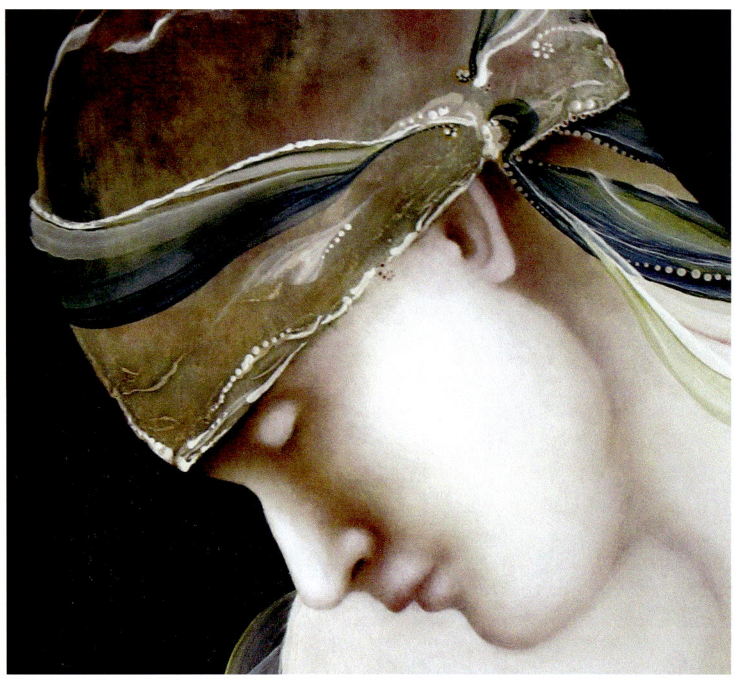

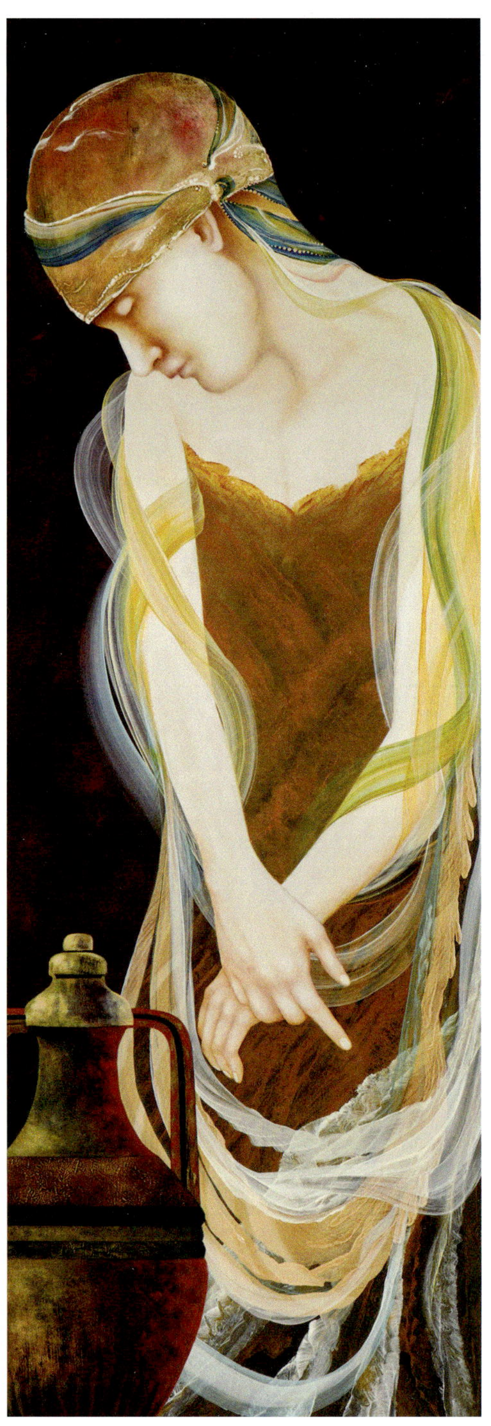

Griffith, Tom.
2006. Oil on wood. 24 in. x 72 in.
Author's personal collection.

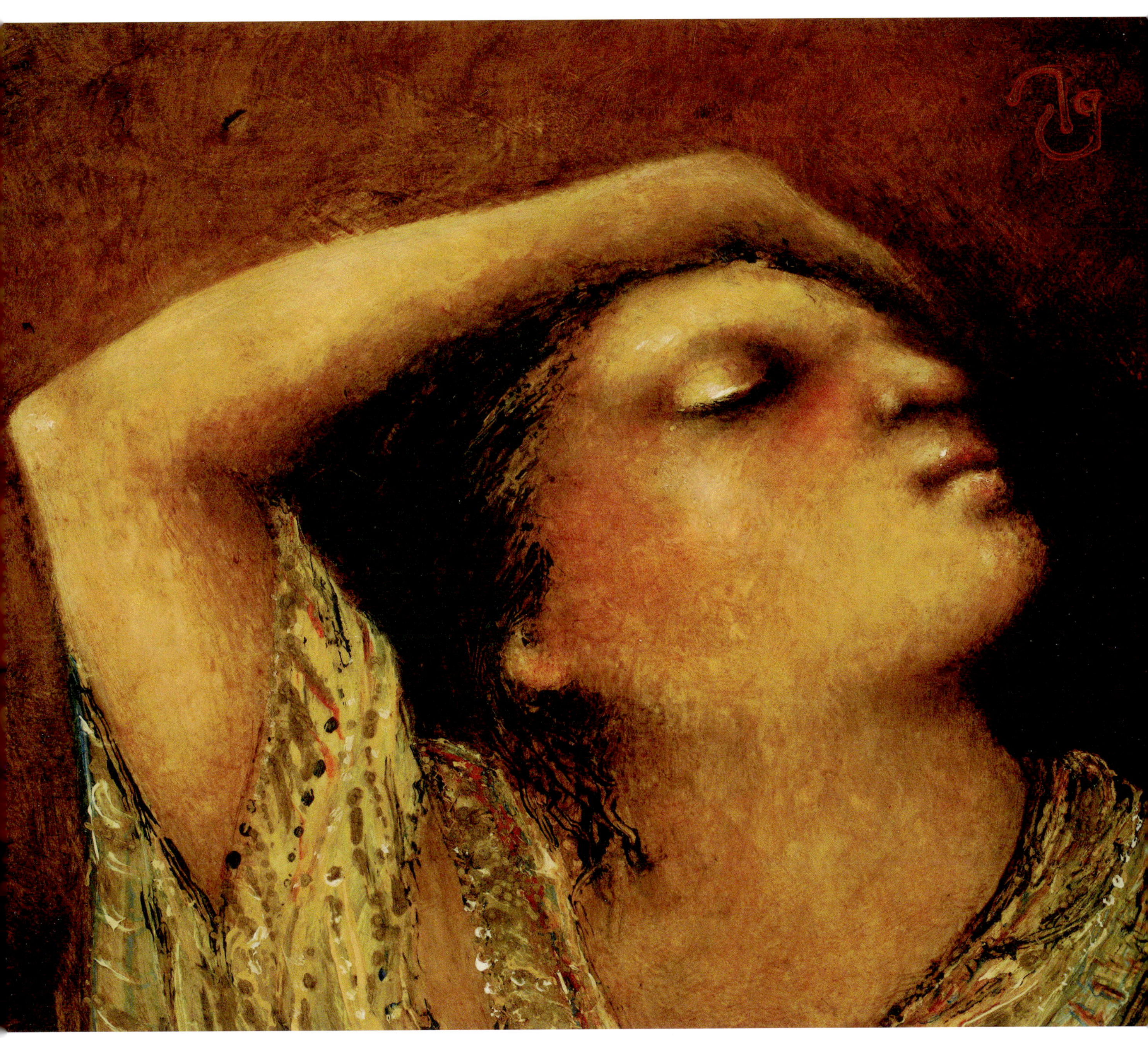

Griffith, Tom.
1999. Oil on wood. 6 in. x 6 in.
Author's personal collection.

THE PALETTE

The colors an artist chooses for their palette are personal and develop and change over time.

My favorite artist was Jan Vermeer of Delft, the Netherlands (1632–1675). At just forty-three when he died (leaving behind a wife and eleven children), Vermeer was almost completely unknown to the art world until the late 1800s. He was a master at expressing light and dark (chiaroscuro) on the human face. Vermeer, unlike most artists (who used blues), almost always used a green glaze over his facial flesh tones of pink to create shadows. Early in the artist's career, Vermeer's "green" was believed to have been a copper green pigment called verdigris, but later in his life (short though it was), he washed over his faces with earth green. Earth green was a color used previously by the Italians. However, the earth green that the Flemish artists used a was much stronger green, achieved by a coarse, more granular pigment.

A typical Dutch palette from the seventeenth century might have included:
lead white
yellow and red ochre
earth green
vermilion
ivory or bone black
lead-tin yellow
madder and carmine lake
raw and burnt sienna
raw and burnt umber
azurite
smalt
ultramarine
Venetian red
English red

COLOR

The color of anything is its actual hue combined with all the light and colors of the objects around it.

This section works with many of the common colors used by the Dutch during the seventeenth century in what is referred to as the Dutch Golden Age.

Note: The Eighty Years' War (1568–1648) basically transferred large numbers of people from the south in the Flanders area (Belgium) into northern regions of the Netherlands. The new Dutch Republic brought huge prosperity to the region, including the desire for non-religious (non-Catholic) art by the new upper-middle class, the merchants, and importers. This "new money" class of people wanted secular subjects to be painted, in addition to the countless portraits of themselves, of course.

The Dutch had a very limited palette. Yet almost any color can be made using a few basic colors.

The Dutch are credited with painting the perfect Caucasian flesh tone, using mainly lead white, yellow ochre, and English red. Darker tones and shadows were often, but not always, achieved with a little ultramarine.

Blue is a cool color, and too much of it results in a cold face. Green, on the other hand, is a warmer color and, when blended with surrounding colors, is easier to work with than blue. Get any blue too close to a yellow, and both are lost, resulting in green instead.

Note: I don't believe black should be anywhere on a painter's palette. Why? Because black on the human face makes it appear as a corpse rather than a live human being. Even the darkest part of any face, such as the pupils of the eyes, can easily be painted with olive green and a touch of alizarin crimson. This goes for black backgrounds around a face and the darkest shadows of clothing and draperies. There is no excuse to ever use black paint.

CATEGORIES OF COLOR

Whites, yellows, reds, greens, blues, browns, and blacks.

White is the reflection of all light. Black is the absorption of color and light.

White is not just white, and black is not just black. There are different hues of white and different hues of black.

Here are some of the main colors used and their general descriptions.

Lead white: silver white, coverage opaque, lead carbonate.

Zinc white: cool tone white, lower coverage, less opaque, zinc oxide.

Titanium white: covers well, the choice of most artists today (available to artists after 1920).

Note: The whites of the eyes are not white at all; they are a color composed of white and the colors around them in the room. Additionally, one eye is always whiter than the other in a portrait. The lighter eye is always on the side of the light source in the room. For example, light coming in from a window on one side of the face makes that eye whiter.

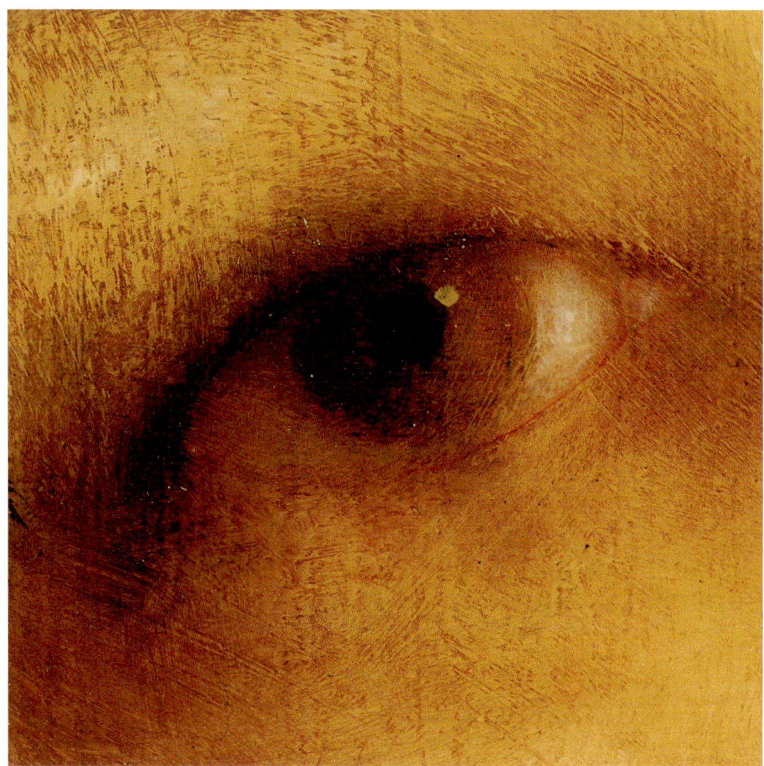

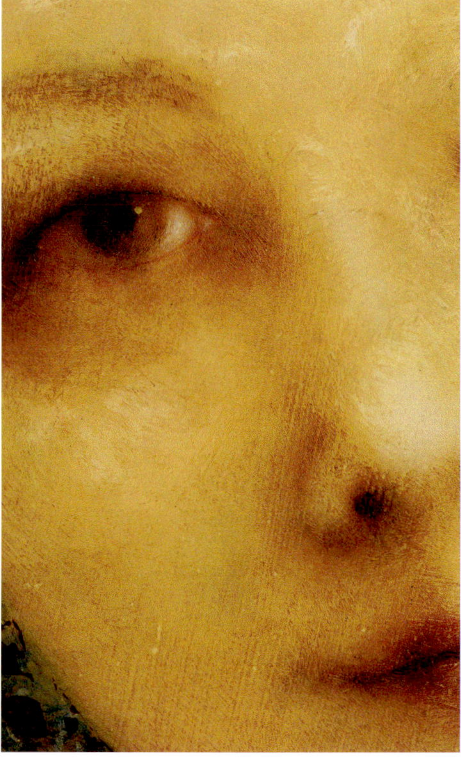

When painting eyes, hard edges (lines) are never a good idea. Hard lines make the eyes look painted. Softness is the key. Thinking of painting eyelashes? Think again. It's not that you can't paint eyelashes; it's my opinion that you shouldn't. I believe it cheapens your work by making the face appear overdone.

Lamp black: cool black, when lightened with white produces a bluish gray.

Ivory black: warm black, a deep dark black that produces a true gray when lightened with white.

Naples yellow: one of the oldest colors used by the great masters (a favorite of Dutch artist Sir Peter Paul Rubens in painting flesh tones). Naples yellow was created by the ancient Egyptians and is one of the original synthetic pigments (since the fifteenth century). Its original form came from natural earth from Mount Vesuvius in Italy. It is often made from lead antimoniate.

Ultramarine: made from a pulverized semi-precious stone, lapis lazuli. A very pretty blue stone, yet rare and very expensive in the time of the *Golden Age*. Using ultramarine in any painting tended to increase the perceived value of that painting to a potential buyer. Latin for "beyond the sea," lapis lazuli was first brought over by the Italians from what is now Afghanistan during the fourteenth and fifteenth centuries. However, it has been used in art since the thirteenth century. When financial circumstances grew thin, ultramarine was the first pigment to leave the palette of an artist. Artists would often stretch out the precious pigment by adding silicon.

Venetian red: almost entirely made of ferric oxide, a natural earth clay called Venetian because for centuries the clay came from a quarry near Venice, Italy; however, the best comes from northern Turkey.

Olive green: a very dark, semi-transparent green made from the chlorophyll of plants. Many variations of this color exist. Most are made from tones of yellow ochre (along with red and blues) and just a touch of black. More than any of the Dutch artists, Vermeer used green extensively as a transparent glaze on the faces he painted, in contrast to blues used by other artists of the day. Like Vermeer, I remain in the "green" camp.

Alizarin crimson: a dye made from the root of the madder plant, used since ancient Egypt, transparent, also known to come from coal-tars. Other crimsons include scarlet, red, yellow, and violet.

Vermilion: red mercuric (mercury) sulphide (sulphur) made from the mineral cinnabar, a commonly produced pigment in the Netherlands in the seventeenth century.

Lead-tin yellow: a combination of lead and tin oxides, commonly used in the seventeenth century by Dutch artists, Rembrandt in particular.

Carmine lake: made from the scales of the beetle called cochineal, red in color. Lake pigments are the combination of a process between dyes and metallic salts.

Smalt: a beautiful blue, which is ground blue potassium glass containing cobalt. Basically, it is two-thirds ground glass (silica) and cobalt oxide. Often used in art for clothing, robes, and draperies. Again, a favorite of Rembrandt.

Green earth: used for centuries, composed of a mixture of the minerals celadonite and glauconite, often with other minerals.

Azurite: the beautiful blue mineral (oxidized copper carbonate) found all over the world and used as a paint pigment since the ancient Egyptians. Azurite was very popular among artists between the fifteenth and eighteenth centuries. On rare occasions, azurite is found in green.

Umber: an unusually dark brown earth pigment made of iron oxide and manganese oxide. Burnt umber produces a very dark brown.

Sienna: a yellowish earth pigment made of iron oxide and manganese oxide. Burnt sienna produces a reddish-brown.

LESSON

Although my palette is very limited in that faces are all I really do, an individual artist's palette should be expanded with at least the basics. There is no need to go out and buy fifty colors to be "ready for anything." Remember that just a handful of colors can produce any color desired.

GENERAL OUTLINE OF THE ALL-ENCOMPASSING PALETTE

Include a selection of opaque or solid colors (non-transparent): Venetian red, yellow ochre light, and cobalt blue light (notice these colors are close to some main base colors of red, yellow, and blue).

Include a selection of transparent colors: alizarin crimson (also known as permanent alizarin, alizarin permanent, crimson madder and madder lake), viridian green, transparent oxide brown, and transparent oxide red.

OBSERVATION

When lightening colors, the simplest way is to add white. But simple is not always best. White is seen as a cool color, and when lightening warm colors such as red and yellow, all that is needed is to mute the intensity of the color being lightened.

For example, to mute the color of red, try adding a touch of a dark green or brown. To lighten red, mix in a little cadmium yellow. To tone down a bright red, add yellow ochre, which is brownish yellow.

Try to avoid adding white to lighten a color, as adding too much white to red, for instance, results in pink. Rather, pick another color to lighten it. The resulting color can be awesome and often surprising.

Hint: Start off with mid-range colors, like ochres, Venetian red, or Naples yellow. When going for realistic portrayals of a subject, most things in life or nature tend to fall into the mid-range colors.

Point: It is always best to portray an atmosphere of moderate lighting. If the light source of a painting is too bright, objects tend to get washed out and detail lost. Conversely, darkness—allowing for the focus to be strictly on the subject—often leaves an artist with a lot of empty board or canvas in the shadows. Avoid focusing all effort and application to the main subject. The periphery and background matter as well. One failure of many artists is that they complete a portraiture and only then start coming up with other "stuff" to fill the surrounding areas.

FAVORITE COLORS

Whether consciously or subconsciously, artists have a color or colors that they like to work with. Sometimes those colors are part of their "signature," a sign that tells everyone, "Yes, that's one of mine." Normally the color(s) selected often have more to do with paintings the artist has done in the past that worked out well, or one that people seem to identify with an artist.

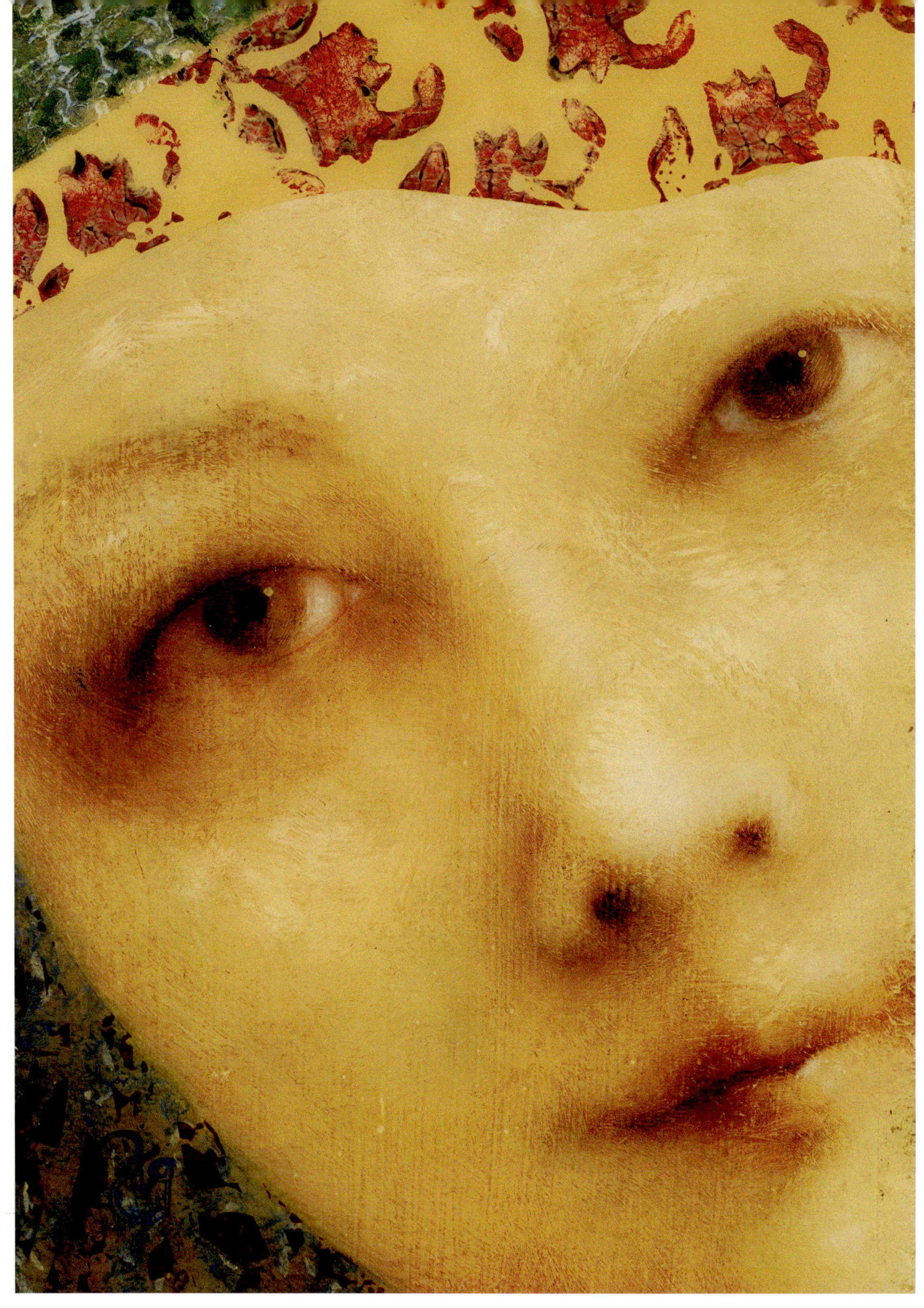

Griffith, Tom.
2014. Oil on wood. 4.5 in. x 6.5 in.
Author's personal collection.

PIGMENTS

Pigments, as opposed to dyes, tend to be inorganic compounds and are generally insoluble in water. From prehistoric man throughout the ages up to modern times, pigments have been added to an artist's palette. Many a forgery has been proven inauthentic when certain pigments (colors) in the forged painting were disclosed to have not been available at the time the authentic work was originally painted.

OCHRE

Natural earth minerals, clay, and silica containing iron oxide used to make pigments for oil paint, such as red ochre, yellow ochre, and brown ochre. Yellow ochre has been used for centuries as a favorite color of many artists, mainly for its ability to mix with other colors to produce a third color.

MADDER

A pigment extracted from the root of the madder plant *(Rubia tinctorum)* to produce such colors as crimson madder and madder lake.

CADMIUM

A heavy metal used to create bright and intense pigments, particularly yellows, oranges, and reds. Discovered about 1820 and used by artists starting around 1845.

LAKE

A method to extract pigment using a salting process, producing such colors as blue lake, red lake, carmine lake, and purple lake. Lakes are a pigment that has been made from a dye by combining that dye with a metallic salt.

OXIDE

Colors made from the compound iron oxide, such as yellow oxide, red oxide, and brown oxide.

SIENNA

A reference to a type of reddish-brown pigment originally from Siena, Italy. An earth pigment containing both manganese and iron oxide. Various colors can be created: yellowish-brown when raw (raw sienna), warm brown when burnt (burnt sienna).

LAPIS LAZULI

A deep blue semi-precious stone used as a pigment to make ultramarine oil paint. Throughout most of art history, lapis lazuli was the most expensive pigment an artist could buy.

UMBER (UMBRA)

A reddish-brown earth pigment containing manganese and iron oxide. From the Latin word *umbra* meaning shadow. When burned, it becomes darker and is called burnt umber. Umbria is a mountainous region in Italy where the pigment was originally extracted.

COLOR

Color is what the brain perceives when the eye takes in light that is either absorbed or reflected off the observed object.

PRIMARY LIGHT COLORS

Red, Green, and Blue. Called the RGB color system. Also referred to as the "colors of light." Although these three colors have been established as the three primary colors, there is still quite a controversy in discussions on color theory. I have read many books on color theory and have been left more confused than when I started. Colors produced by light are classified differently than those in the printing industry. Thus, the difference in the use of the word "primary" colors versus "primary pigment" colors. Basically, the human optical system signals only three hues of color to the brain: red, green, and blue.

SECONDARY LIGHT COLORS

These are the primary pigment colors. Secondary light colors are accomplished by mixing any two of the primary light colors: blue light plus green light creates cyan. Red light plus blue light creates magenta. Green light plus red light creates yellow. Note: cyan, magenta, and yellow, plus black stand for CMYK, which are the only four colors used in the printing industry.

COMPLEMENTARY LIGHT COLORS

Red is the complement of cyan.
Green is the complement of magenta.
Blue* is the complement of yellow.

*Even though violet (purple) is the complement of mid-range yellows.

COMPLEMENTARY COLORS

A color's opposite on the color wheel. Used primarily for determining what color to mix with something's tonal (actual) color to create a shadow. Note: My definition here is purposely short. The actual definition of a complementary color varies and can get complicated.

COLOR WHEEL

A circle, though sometimes a grid, of colors that shows the relationships between primary colors, secondary colors, and tertiary colors.

PRIMARY PIGMENT COLORS

Cyan blue, Magenta, and Yellow. No combination of colors can make a primary pigment color. (CMYK is in reference to the color of inks used in digital printing; the 'K' stands for black). Any color can be created using these four inks in the printing and art world.

TERTIARY COLORS

Colors mixed from the pigmented primary colors of cyan, magenta, and yellow—namely, light green, emerald green, ultramarine, scarlet, violet, and orange.

LOCAL COLOR

The actual color of an object. An apple is red. A banana is yellow.

REFLECTED COLOR

The color of another object bouncing its hue onto the object being painted.

TONAL COLOR

A mix of the local color and the color of the objects around it (very important when painting still life, such as bowls of fruit).

VALUES/TONES

The range of lightness to darkness of any single color. A scale from white to black is a perfect example. Flemish artists (the Dutch) are said to have had a range of nine tones for every color. These consisted of four light tones, three dark tones, and two middle tones. However, they would typically only use five of the nine tones in a single painting.

For practice purposes, take any four sets of colors and mix them together. Place four colors at the top and four at the bottom. Mix different ratios of one color into the other and observe the result. In this case, we have from left to right: cadmium yellow light and oxide of chromium green, cobalt blue and Venetian red, cadmium yellow deep hue and Naples yellow, and French ultramarine and cerulean blue.

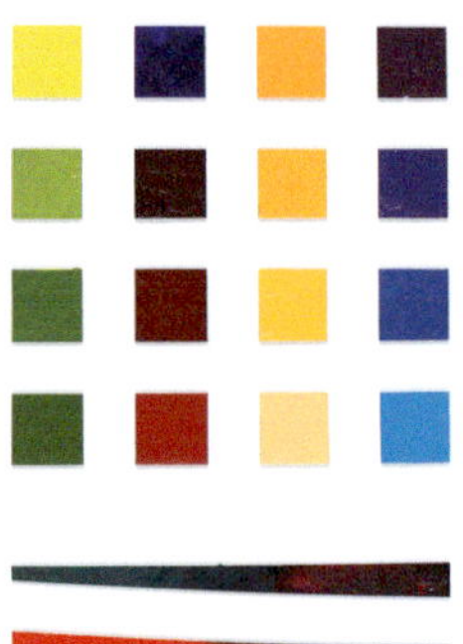

TOO MUCH, TOO MUCH!

The painting below demonstrates the danger in getting too carried away with finishing glaze coats. Specifically, changing the colors of the multiple layers of glazes. The result is an unnatural rainbow of colors that represents the painting more as a cartoon than a fine work of art.

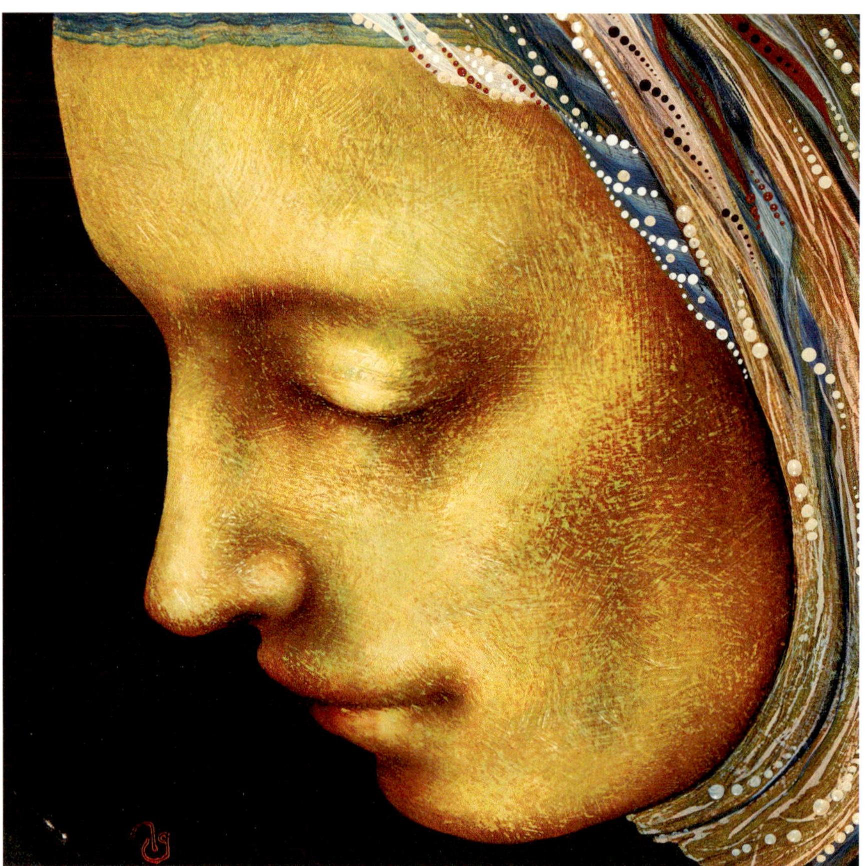

Griffith, Tom.
1997. Oil on wood. 14 in. x 14 in.
Author's personal collection.

NOTABLES

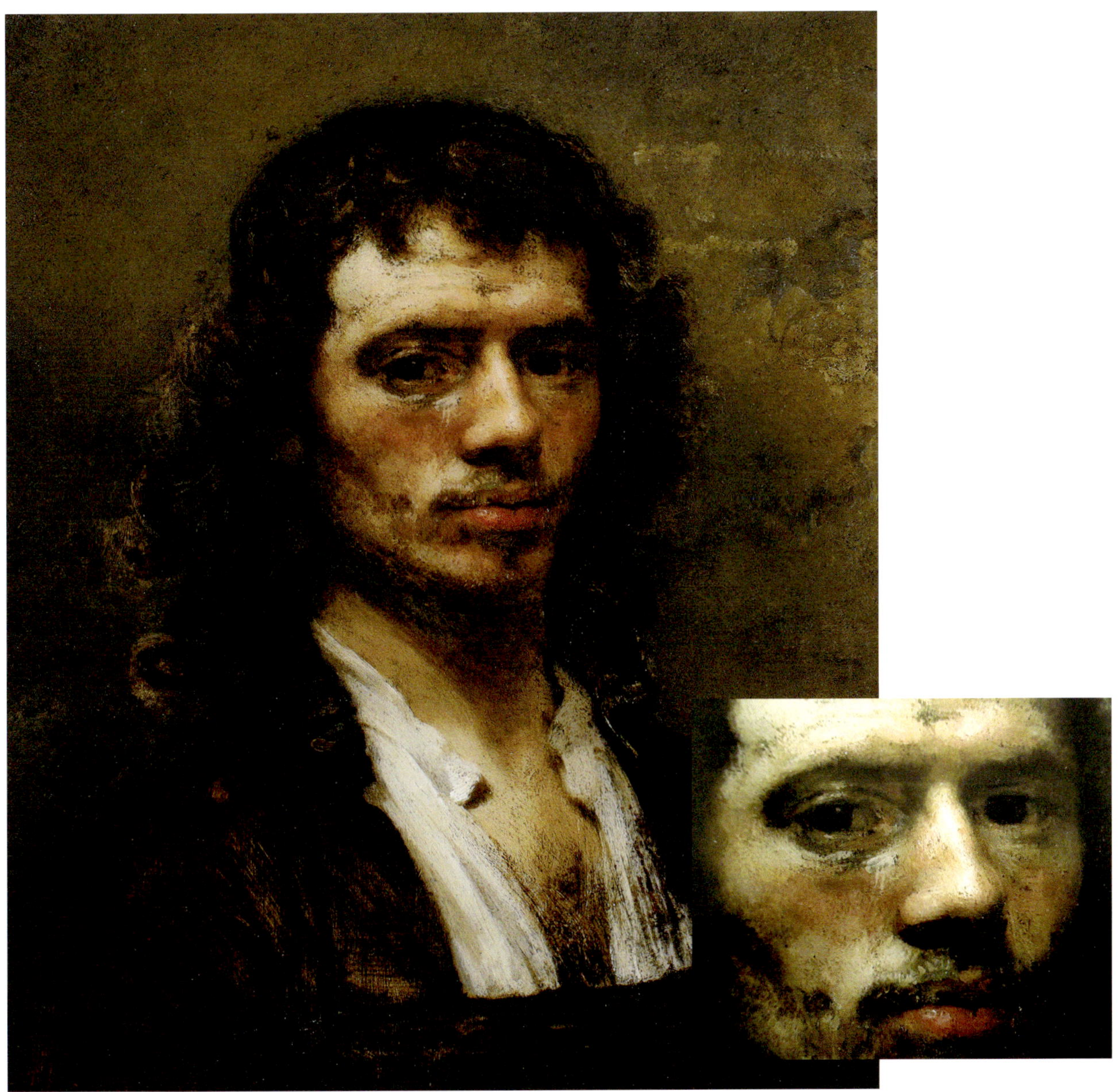

Fabritius, Carel.
Self-Portrait. 1645.
Museum Boijmans Van Beuningen, Rotterdam, the Netherlands.
(Rembrandt's most promising student, and most likely Vermeer's teacher. Killed at the age of thirty-two in a gunpowder explosion in Delft, the Netherlands, also the hometown of Vermeer.)

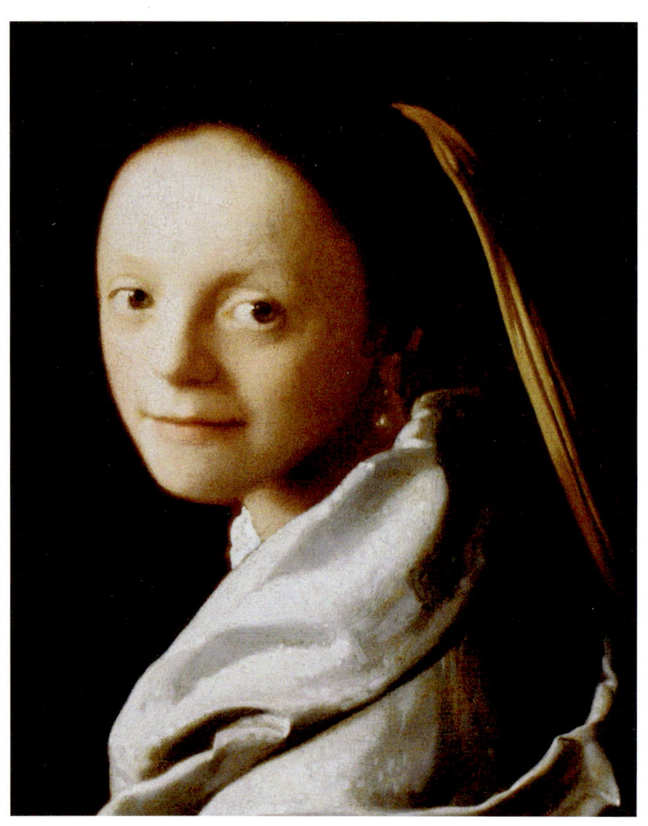

Vermeer
(1632–1675)
Mysterious Genius

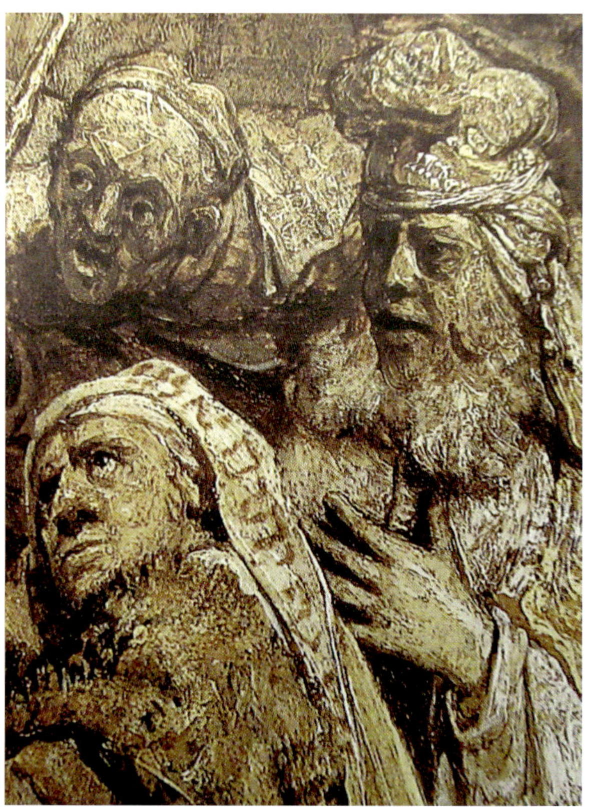

Rembrandt
(1606–1669)
The Greatest Rebel

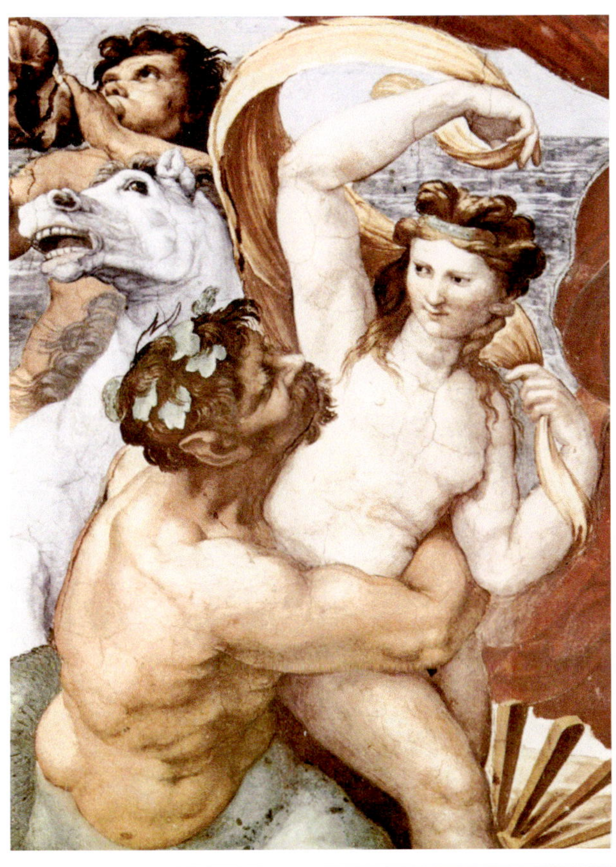

Raphael
(1483–1520)
Neoplatonic Grandeur

Titian
(1488–1576)
Venetian Art Master

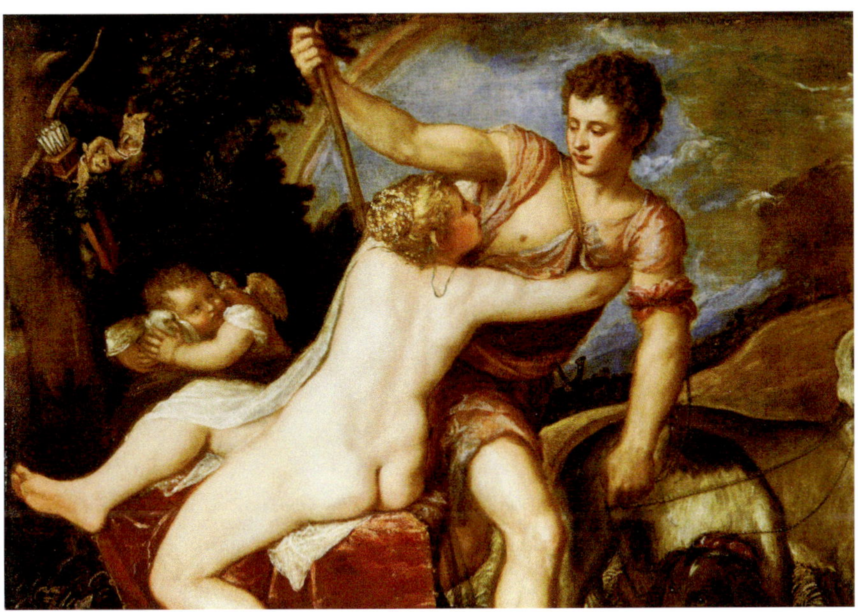

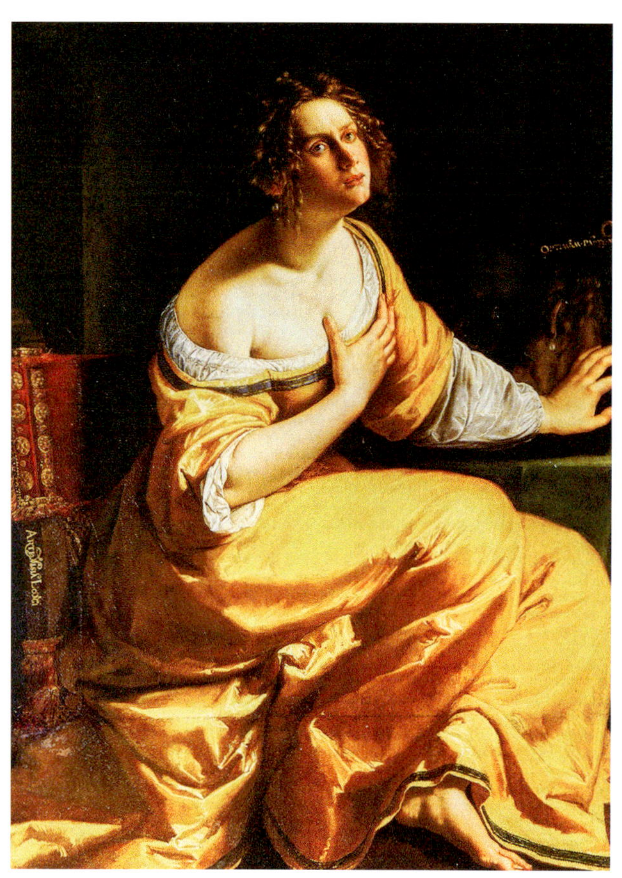

Gentileschi
(1593–1653)
Her Greatness

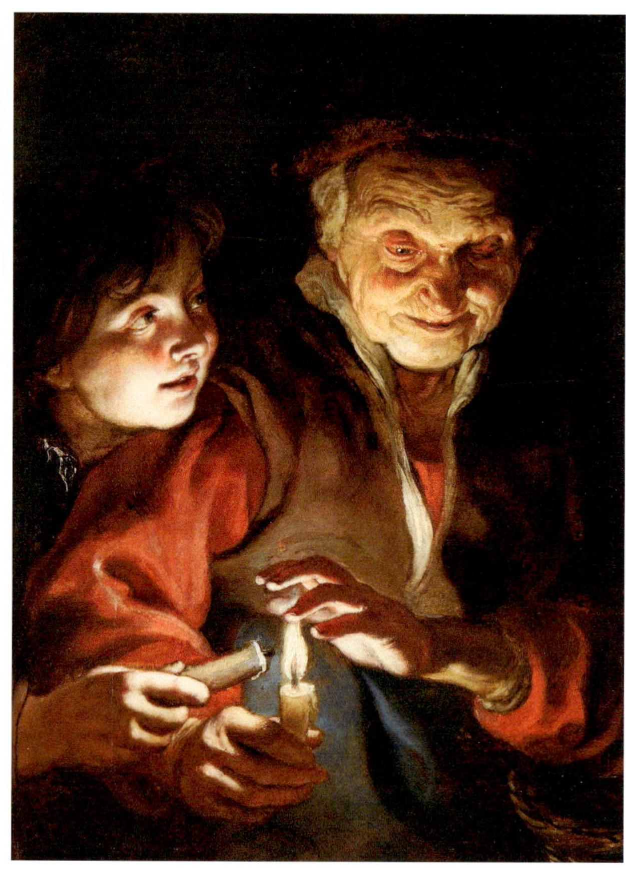

Rubens
(1577–1640)
Flemish Baroque Master

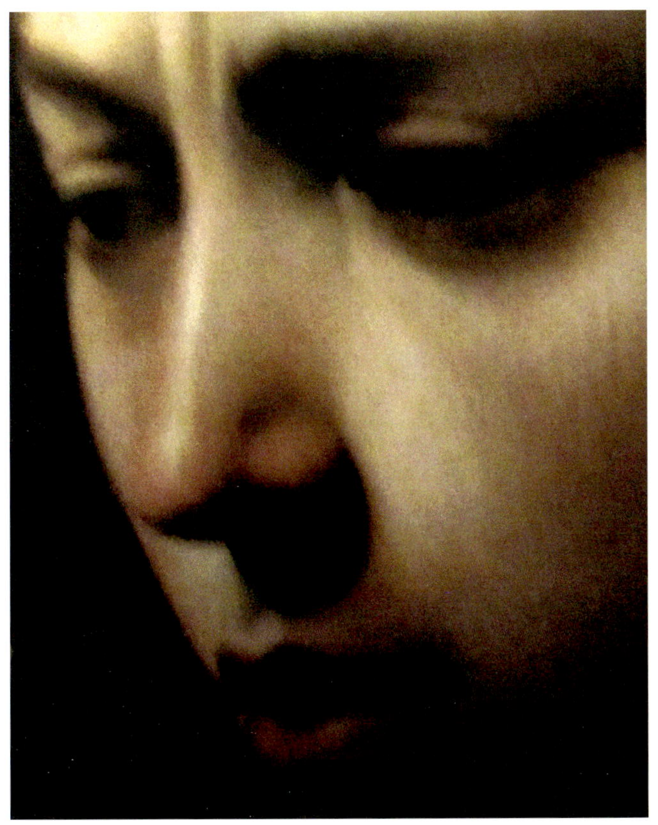

Caravaggio
(1571–1610)
Baroque Tenebrist, Definition of a Master

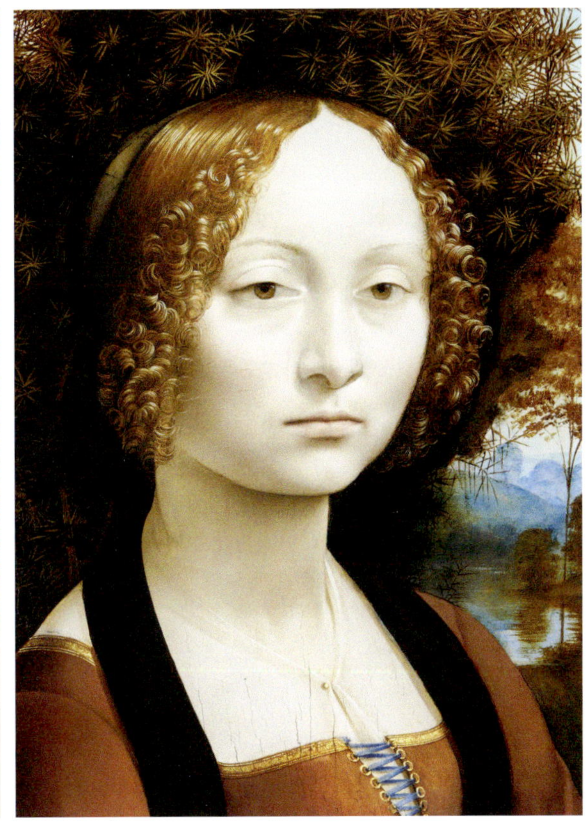

da Vinci
(1452–1519)
Renaissance Man

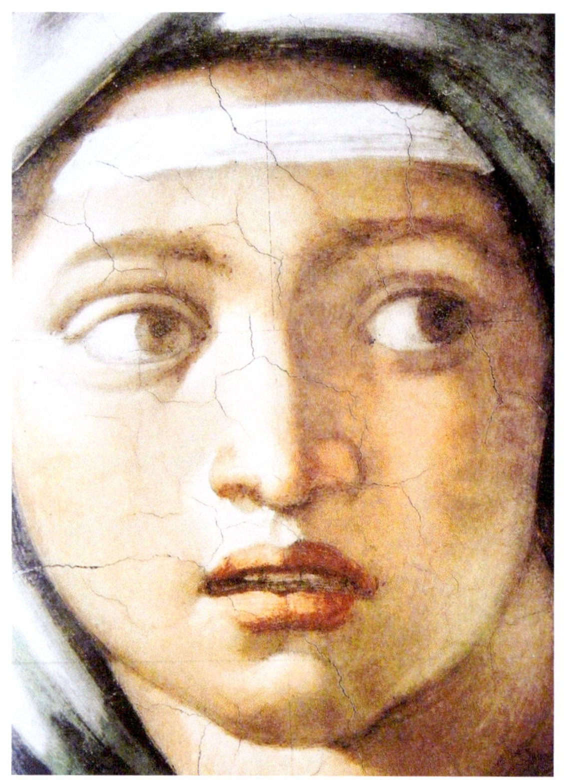

Michelangelo
(1475–1564)
Polymath Master

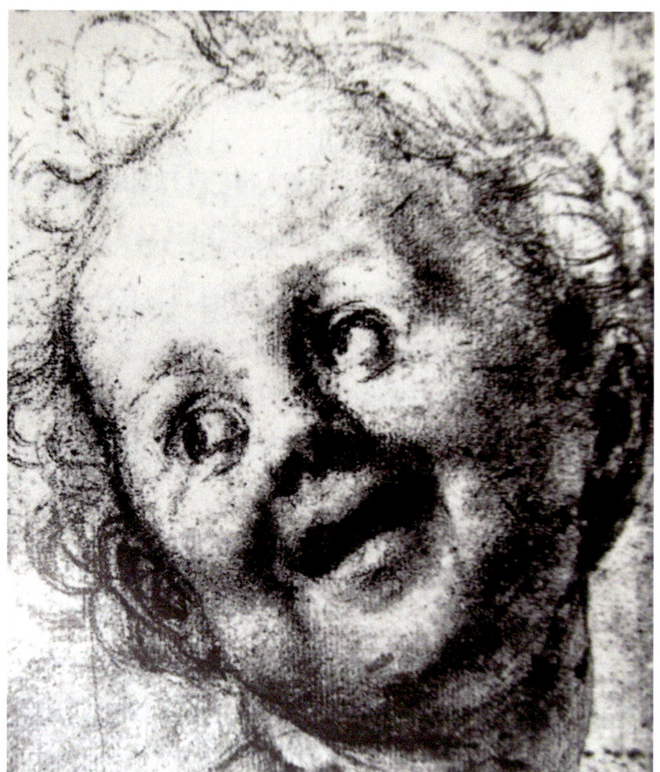

Pontormo
(1494–1557)
Those Marble Eyes

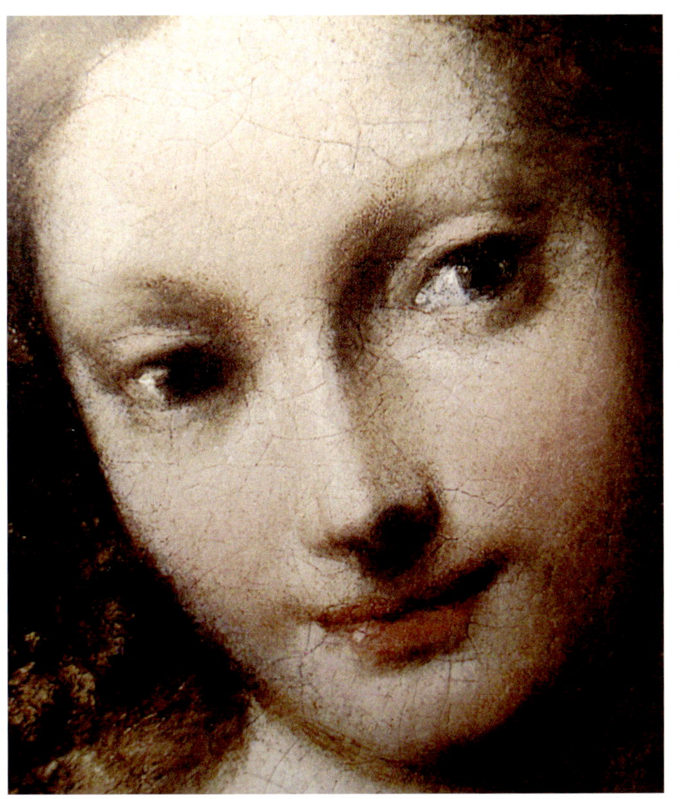

da Correggio
(1489–1534)
Parma School Master

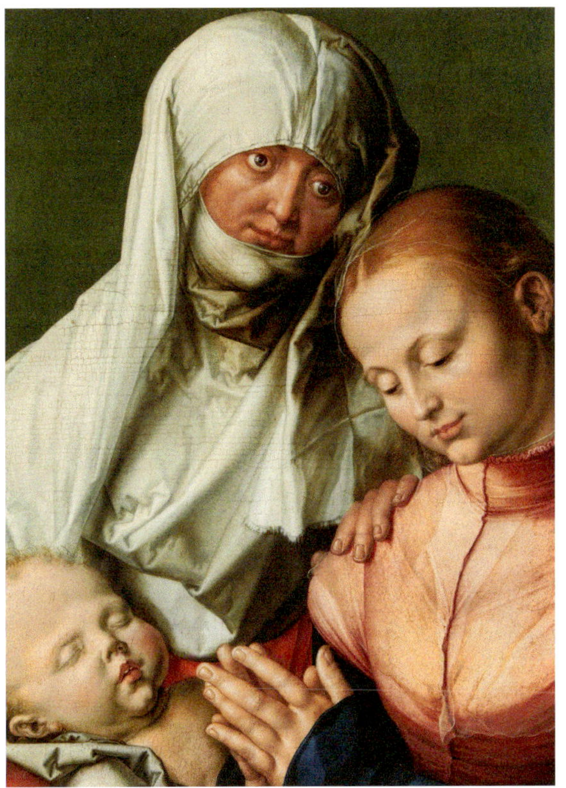

Dürer
(1471–1528)
Germany's Most Notable

CLOSING

In closing, it is my sincere hope that the information in this book helps developing painters better understand the thought process involved in painting the human face. Artists will throw away ten paintings before ever framing one. The more one studies the paintings of those who have come before them, the more one realizes that overwhelming detail is not necessary to achieve the desired results. Close observation will reveal that many of the greatest faces ever painted were simple instead of detailed and complex. The mastery of the work is in how the artist demonstrated the use of light and shadow, proportionality, color, expression, and technique with their pigments and brush.

Sometimes the hardest thing about oil painting
is putting down enough paint to
cover up the numbers.

—Tom Griffith

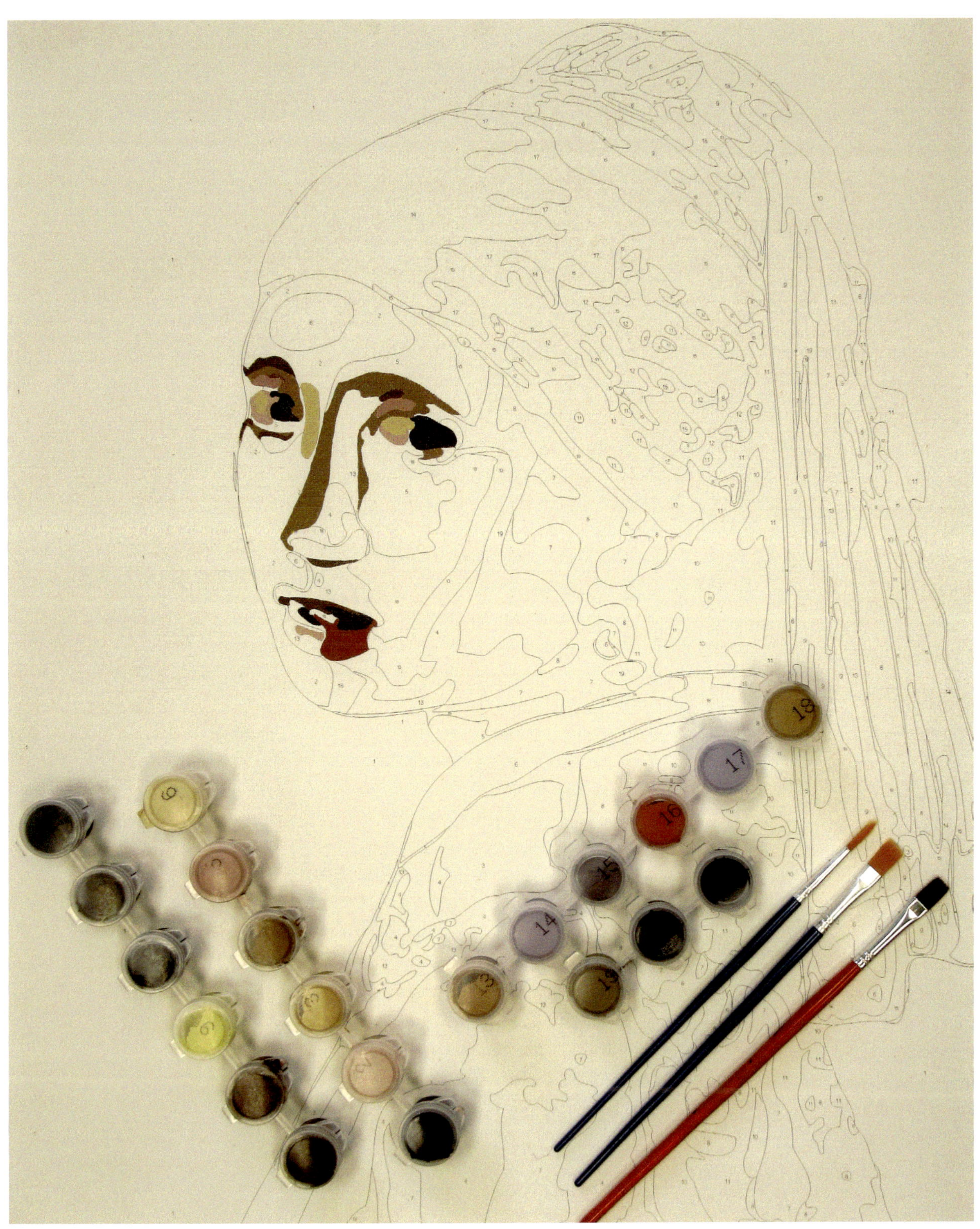

AUTHOR'S NOTE

Being a loner as a young man, I would have thought that all that free time would have produced mountains of creativity, and that creativity would have lent itself to painting better pictures. Not true. In fact, what it did was provide me the opportunity to look for other creative outlets on which to spend that time. The time spent trying various artistic mediums such as watercolors and acrylics really pushed me toward the end result of oil painting. Gravitating to oils was something I never thought I could achieve. At first it appeared that the knowledge necessary to paint a realistic human face was too daunting to absorb and master.

I learned was that in oil painting, one never "masters" anything. Rather, we just get a little better as we complete one more painting.

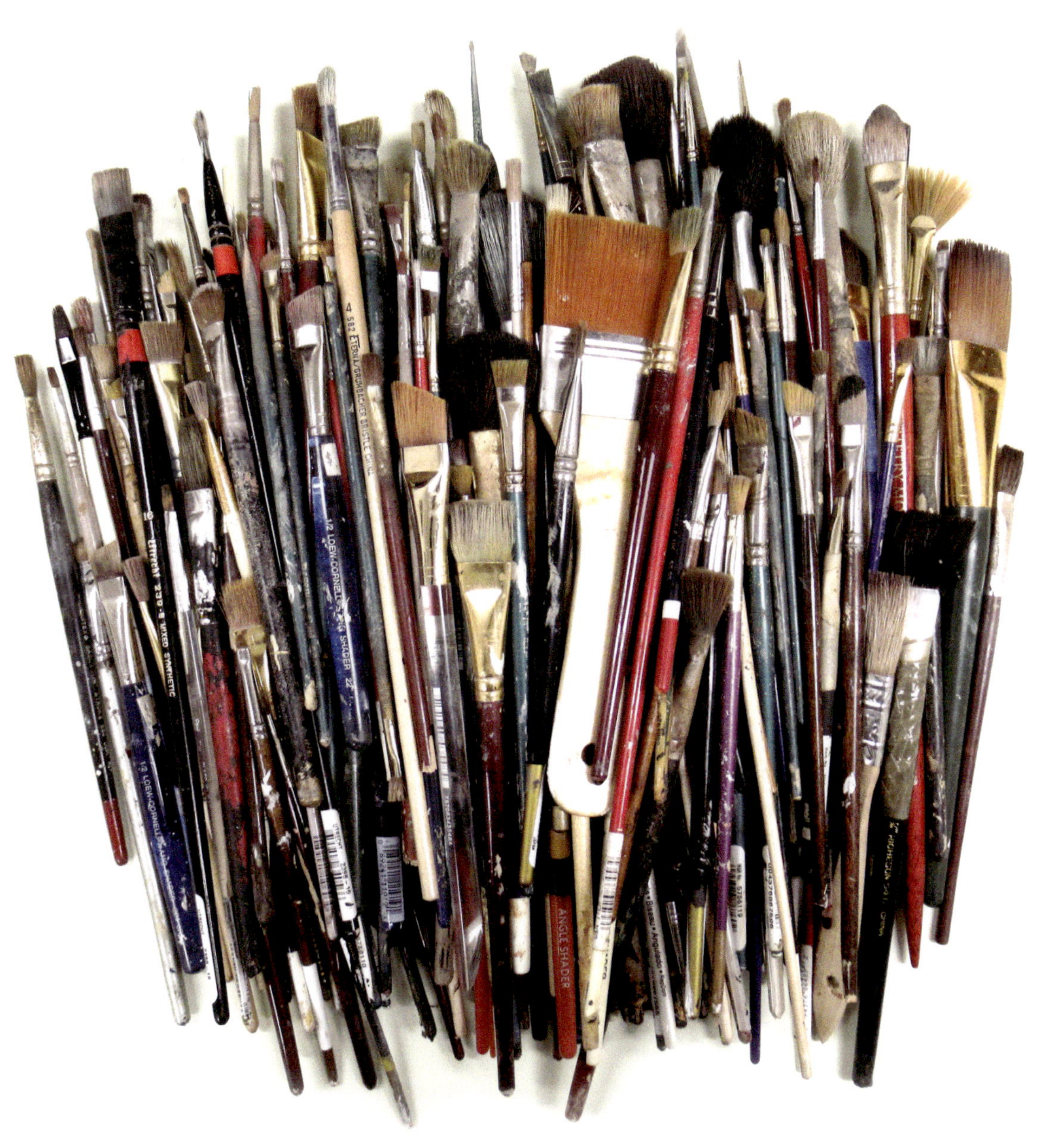

Forty years of painting.

A handful of paintings good enough to be framed.

Lots of trial and error, mostly error.

300 old brushes to prove you made the journey!

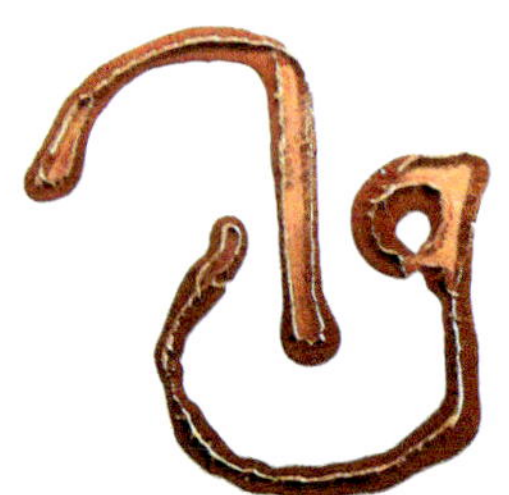